Searched Me
Out and
Known Me

'In this Lenten companion, Charlie takes us through our human frailties, questions, challenges, and joys through the lens of the Psalter. With searing hope he offers us a reflective tool kit to enter the journey to the cross with renewed purpose. Of all the seasons in the church year, Lent perhaps is the one that offers the most to a world hungry for God with little sense of how to connect. The poetry of the Psalms, with praise and lament, provides such a vehicle. Charlie shows us how these most ancient of words and songs resonate with the rawness of our humanity in the present. The reflections in this book offer a firm nudge to those who might need it, and a purposeful comfort where that is most felt. You cannot read this book and not pause to reflect. You cannot reach its end without exploring afresh what it is to truly be a disciple of Jesus. I suspect this book will become more than a Lenten pilgrimage. May it be a prophetic cry to our church and world today.'

**Rt Revd Dr Helen-Ann Hartley,
Bishop of Newcastle**

'A Lenten book which combines accessibility and lightness of touch with shrewd commentary on the daily Scripture readings in light of contemporary issues, this is a rare find. It works as well for individuals as for groups, offering spiritually robust and honest challenges as well as the opportunity to broaden and deepen personal spiritual horizons. A former chorister's love of the text shines through it and invites the reader to develop their own insights and responses. An excellent companion for Lent.'

Sr Gemma Simmonds CJ

Searched Me Out and Known Me

Journeying Lent with the Psalms

CHARLIE BELL

DARTON · LONGMAN + TODD
INTELLIGENT ◆ INSPIRATIONAL ◆ INCLUSIVE
SPIRITUAL BOOKS

In Memoriam
Lyndon van der Pump

First published in 2024 by
Darton, Longman and Todd Ltd
Unit 1, The Exchange
6 Scarbrook Road
Croydon CR0 1UH

ISBN 978-1-915412-78-2

A catalogue record for this book is available from the British Library.

Designed and produced by Judy Linard

Printed and bound in Great Britain by Short Run Press, Exeter

Contents

Preface

I CANNOT BE THE only person who is secretly quite pleased when Lent comes around again.

Don't get me wrong – the last few weeks and months of celebration and feasting, of Christmas, Epiphany, Candlemas, and carnival, are a very necessary part of the warp and weft of the Christian life, and I wouldn't do without them. Puritanism is just as wrong in the twenty-first century as it ever has been, and getting tired of feasting might well prove a problem when we eventually make it – God willing – to the heavenly Jerusalem. Yet there is something so holy, so necessary, so human about these few weeks of taking a step back, paring things back to the essentials, that really seems to do the soul a whole lot of good. There is something about it which speaks to a deeply felt human need.

Our contemporary world – and even our contemporary church – has somewhat lost sight of the importance of the cyclical nature of life. From simple things, like the travel industry's temptations to us to 'escape the winter months', to our deep fear of illness, frailty, and death, and our hope that if we simply ignore it, it won't happen, our ability to live lives embedded in a regular pattern of change seem endlessly challenged. In our churches, the need to be 'relevant' and to compete with secular Sunday mornings means that even our commitment to weekly worship together has waned significantly. In addition, fewer and fewer churches are offering weekday opportunities to worship, and those that are offered routinely lose out to the busyness and the business of the day-to-day.

Not all of this is, of course, purely bad news. It is simply a fact of life that people's engagement with community life, including communities of faith, is more transient and more fleeting than before. In the church, we can moan and groan about that, or we can quite rightly try to find ways to enable people to experience something of the transcendent, seeking to feed the spiritual hunger that is never too deep beneath the surface. There is a challenge, a tension, really, to this – on the one hand our desire to nourish in a way that can be received, whilst at the same time our hope, our calling, to point people towards the divine. Getting the 'spiritual' right has never been easy, and our time is no exception – and as much as it is a challenge for the church, it is an opportunity, too.

Without wanting to paint too dire a picture, we do need to be honest that the outlook for the church – and this includes my own Church of England – is not looking too rosy, at least if we look at it from some angles. Putting it bluntly, we are simply not replacing the worshippers who are dying year on year – and so we are shrinking in terms of numbers, in terms of influence, and in terms of confidence. Our lack of confidence is sometimes named, and sometimes not – but whether we want to own up to it or not, it sits beneath so much of what we end up doing and being.

It is perhaps this loss of confidence in our future – which is so often a loss of confidence in what *we* can achieve, rather than a reliance on the God of the universe who calls us to participate in what God is already achieving – that sits at the heart of our loss of confidence in who and what we are. Much is said and written about evangelism, but until and unless our church is willing to model and live out a life steeped in the Gospel, it is very unlikely we are going to attract people to such a life. Our seemingly endless desire to make Christianity a little less weird, a little more 'accessible' (to use that terribly overused and under-defined word), means that we run the risk of throwing the baby out with the bathwater. Our apparent unwillingness to be *both* self-critical *and* to respond to the call of the Lord Jesus in St Matthew's Gospel to go and make disciples of all nations means we run the risk of becoming increasingly similar to the world, whilst at the same time losing the ability to speak to that world. We become irrelevant in our desperation for relevance.

In recent years, there has been much focus on our need to be somehow 'counter-cultural' without any serious examination of what that means. Our internal debates, whether about the ordination of women, the blessing of same sex couples, the heresy of racism, or whatever other trigger issue, might have been dressed in ecclesial vestments, but have far too often been little more than worldly debates clad in the Emperor's new clothes. We like to think of ourselves as just a little bit above worldly debates, but far too often we merely add some theological language and end up having precisely the same debates in almost exactly the same way. There has been much talk of modelling things differently – but little success in doing so. At the heart of so much of this is power, and control, and fear, and self-centredness, and doubt, and betrayal – in other words, at the heart of so much of this are the very things Lent calls us to think more deeply upon.

Nor does being truly counter-cultural mean simply choosing something the rest of the world says X on, and belligerently saying Y. Instead, it surely means offering some resistance to the mission creep of twenty-first century cultural assumptions and offering solidarity to those caught up in the swell. It means refusing to play on a playing field designed by 'convenience' and so-called 'choice', and instead making God our starting point. It means making ourselves responsible for the decisions we take and the acts we undertake, and it means an intentional bringing ourselves back to the essentials of what our faith proclaims about the world. In doing so, it means connecting what we believe with the way we live – and the way we try to enable others to live, too.

Let me give you an example. Today's weekends having increasingly become emblematic of our two-tier society. On the one hand, we have people – often wealthier, with more secure jobs – who truly do still have weekends off. That's not to say that their lives aren't stressful, or that weekends are a mere wallowing in the joys of life, but – in theory, at least – they exist. Yet for vast swathes of the population – far more than we might realise – weekends simply do not exist. Shift workers, those working more than one job, factory and shop workers, the list is long, and depressing – with the increasing push towards a 24/7 society, the burden is shouldered by those who are so often the least fortunate, and the least respected, in our communities. Whilst the irritation felt when shops aren't open on Sundays, for example, is somewhat understandable, this irritation is not relieved without human cost.

Now as a church we may simply accept that this is the price of our 24/7 world, throw our hands up in the air and proclaim that all is lost and there is no point fighting it. During the coronavirus pandemic, in the church's stated willingness to 'set an example' to the wider population, we seemed to forget that vast swathes of the population, and our congregations, didn't need to be set an 'example' to stay at home – they were working, day by day, in essential roles, at increased risk of contracting disease and with fewer resources to manage if things went wrong. Alternatively, we can bang on about the 'loss of Christian values', finding any cause – however spurious – to launch increasingly absurd and damaging legal battles, engaging in a finger-wagging public censure campaign in which we come across as moralistic, tiresome, and lacking not only in a sense of humour but in a sense of proportion, too.

Yet simply proclaiming we have nothing to say, or conversely jumping up and down and showing ourselves to be little more than annoying controversialists, are not the only options available to us. There is much in the tradition to draw from, and we have much to offer to conversations on public life. We might start, for example, from our deep theological belief in the dignity of all people, created equally in the image and likeness of God. We might think, too, of the importance of the concept of 'time' in our Christian story and in the wider human experience. We really do have things to say, that challenge and enrichen the wider conversation. We just need to be willing – and equipped – to say them.

Which brings us back to Lent. Because, this Lent, I

want to challenge the pervasive 'it doesn't really matter' mentality, and say – yes, it really does, and particularly when it comes to setting aside time for God (and enabling others to do the same). Worshipping week by week in Lent really does matter. Worshipping day by day during Holy Week really does matter. Preparing for Easter really does matter. In saying so, I'm not pretending away all the other pressures of life, all the many valid reasons that we might all have that make it difficult, but I am suggesting that this is a time of year when our faith needs to be put front and centre. Of course, there will be times and moments when it is simply not possible to give this time to the Lord, or rather where our service to the Lord is found primarily in our service to our neighbours, but there will also be other times and moments when we simply choose not to put the time aside, or where we make choices that make it impossible for others. This is not a clerical guilt trip, and I truly do know how busy life can be – it is, rather, an invitation to reflect a little, and to ask whether our commitment to Christ might need a reshaping of our priorities every once in a while.

The church hasn't always modelled this way of being terribly successfully. The decline in the focus on the liturgical year in many of our churches, and the continued suspicion of taking Holy Week 'too seriously' is a key example of this. 'Every Sunday is Easter Sunday' is a better soundbite than pastoral aid – of course it is true that each Sunday we celebrate the resurrection of the Lord Jesus, including every Sunday of Lent, yet it is also true that taking time to intentionally walk our way through the church year, remembering the events of Jesus' life in a way that moves beyond mere recollection, is not only a powerful spiritual discipline but a particular way of hallowing time. In our desire not to appear too 'weird' or unworldly, and in our keenness to simplify some of the elaborate parts of the Christian tradition, we run the risk of letting go of something quite precious. As ever – and I would say this as an Anglican – there is a *via media*!

Similarly, talking about 'time' is not value neutral. On occasion, the powerful in our church and in our society have demanded that others, very often those with rather less power and privilege, 'bide their time', 'are patient', 'show restraint'. This might sound benign, yet this far too frequently ends up being a way of silencing minority voices or demanding those already facing injustice wait just a little longer for those with power to take it seriously and act. Wherever we find ourselves situated in the world or the church, we need to be alert to quite what demands we put on others when it comes to *their* time – and what demands God might be putting on us when it comes to *our* time.

Lent is one of those seasons of the church's year which gives us a bit of an opportunity to get off the bandwagon, do some of the deep thinking, and re-situate ourselves within the divine life to which we are called. For far too long, Lent has been seen as a time of misery – a time of ashen faces, denying ourselves, and being generally a bit dour. Ash and denial are not necessarily a bad thing, but the wider public understanding of Lent as being a time for Christians to be even more miserable than usual does us no favours at all! Lent, rather, is a time for being open to the abundance and generosity of God, a time of preparation for the extraordinary Feast of Easter, and a time to regain some of the spiritual gifts that can ensue from good and healthy spiritual discipline. It is a time of renewal, and of hope – a time of rediscovering the love of God in our lives and in the lives of others – and it is a time when our willingness to ask questions, in faith, can deepen and widen our own small glimpse of the vision of holiness. It is a time when our stripped back lives give us the opportunity to look for the signs of the times and at the same time to listen again to the call of God. In doing so, it might just give us the voice to speak, too.

So in approaching Lent this year, I invite you to think deeply about the role of time in your life, and in the lives of those around you. Everything in modern life is in short supply – we have to make endless and sometimes quite painful choices about what we prioritise, and how we prioritise it. Those choices can relate to money, to resources more generally, to our energies, to our friendships and relationships. Yet at the heart of so many of these choices is our time – and how we choose, or feel compelled, to spend it. Will we take on that extra bit of work to help us pay the bills, or will we give up that Sunday afternoon to spend with a lonely acquaintance? Will we go to church, or will we use Sunday morning to spend some precious time with the family – or even to catch up on the sleep that we are all so in need of?

It is a truism that the church calls us to a different way of being, yet this different way of being takes work, and can provide us with more tensions and challenges rather than fewer. Not only is there the tension between service to God and service to others, but there is also the very real call to give enough time and attention to the self, not to selfishly massage our egos or follow the somewhat banal overtures of the self-help industry, but to spend a

14

little time in the presence of God and learn a little more about ourselves. This can, of course, be time spent before the Blessed Sacrament, or in prayer, but it can be time, too, spent in recreation and leisure. Whilst our society offers more and more opportunities for leisure, we still seem – somewhat bizarrely – to look down on those who take advantage of those opportunities. Taking a break, enjoying the world God has given us, is far too often seen as something suspect and not quite the done thing. 'What did you get up to over the weekend?' is all too frequently asked in censorious terms, as if the answer 'well, not terribly much really' is not quite acceptable. Our obsession with being productive, our need to be seen to be achieving something, makes leisure seem an excuse or a pointless pastime.

Yet our refusal to embrace leisure ourselves so often has an impact on others, too. The self-denial of leisure amongst middle class, well-off folk, so often means that leisure in those less well-off is seen as somehow unnecessary, as problematic, as 'undeserved'. In each generation, the concept of the 'undeserving poor' is never too far beneath the surface, and in our own it surely makes itself known in the way so many of us bristle if benefits money is spent on things for pure pleasure. How dare these people, and it is always *these people*, because it is far easier to demonise without giving someone a name and an identity, how dare these people waste their money? How dare they waste their time?

Of course, while we deny others their leisure time, we still surreptitiously take our own. There is no widespread condemnation of holiday travel, or expensive meals out with friends. We might feel a bit guilty about taking them, but at the same time we can convince ourselves that we 'deserve' them nonetheless. We might be appalled by the profligacy of others, but after all our hard work, don't we deserve a few moments of rest and recuperation? Yet in our own desperation to be productive, we risk working ourselves into the ground, and hence displacing any possible leisure from this recuperation – turning ourselves into little more than workhorses put out to pasture every few months to regain the strength to once again take on the yoke.

To return to God for a moment, this is surely not that for which we were created. The biblical narrative is not one whereby God's plan is worked out in all work and no play – there is a reason the Sabbath was instituted, even if we routinely ignore it in our twenty-first century-freneticism (which, by the way, is a sin!). In our lives, we are called to a pattern of work and play, to worship of God and to loving service of God's world. We are not, and were not created as, machines – we are the image and likeness of God. That 'we', of course, reminds us that what is true for us is true for all.

The contemporary church does, it must be said, occasionally opine about 'simply being and not doing', but these exhortations so often appear to come from a totally unworldly fantasy world that the best that can be done with them is for them to be ignored. The church continues, all too frequently, to be a creature of the middle class, where middle class assumptions, opportunities, and biases are taken to be matters-of-fact of Christian life. In its worst excesses, we see the rich giving the money, and the poor doing the work – yet even where this kind of crass classism is not in existence, still we accept the fact that poorer parishes, less shiny and less well resourced, should be allowed to struggle, whilst the rich, well-to-do, and glitzy parishes refuse to pay more than their 'rightful dues' to the church's finances.

So when we hear about 'being and not doing', this all too infrequently ignores the fact that for those who are struggling to make ends meet, this is simply not doable – it's not possible. There is a particular cruelty to demanding people 'just be', when they can only just about manage as it is. Our failure as a church to see our challenge in this area as requiring us not only to be prophetic in what we call individuals to, but also to be prophetic in how we challenge society to enable this, is stark, and deeply problematic. We cannot merely try to make changes in our own lives – we need to be committed to societal change, too, to enable others to do the same. 'Truly I tell you, just as you did it to one of the least of these brothers and sisters of mine, you did it to me.'

With this in mind, the observation of Lent can, it seems, fall into two traps. The first of these is to see it as a time of spiritual renewal, the gifts, opportunities, and richness of which can then be jettisoned for the rest of the church year. A time of spiritual renewal it is, but a time where this renewal *changes* us, resets us in a fundamental way that has an impact for the rest of the year. It is a time of preparation, and not a time of stepping away from the rest of our lives. It is, in other words, a time to give ourselves a good shake, shut up, and listen to what God might have to say to us about our whole selves.

The second mistake is to turn this into yet another period of self-improvement for the privileged, in the process making it essentially impossible for many people to take part. This kind of Lent, which is dressed in the language of self-help, is quite simply not what this is all about. Lent is not, of course, about anything *we* do, but about what God does, and God doesn't demand or expect of us those things that would harm our wellbeing. For some of us, then, Lent will be calling us not only to interrogate and resituate our own priorities as they relate to ourselves, but also our engagement with the wider world. We might ask ourselves not only whether changes need to be made in our own lives, but how we might contribute to changing society so that others might have the freedom to make the same changes. Our calling as Christians is not individualistic – it is communal. As my bishop, the Bishop of Southwark, puts it, 'we are saved together or we are not saved at all'.

This way of conceiving of our own privilege is not an attempt to 'guilt trip' or to make ourselves miserable and self-flagellate. Instead, it is an attempt to look at the world as it really is, rather than as we might pretend it is, and in so doing, to commit ourselves to the freedom and grace that God promises to *all* God's people. We are not voiceless, uninvolved observers in the Kingdom of Heaven – we are intricately and inextricably bound up, one with another. As we travel the road to Calvary, and as we travel the road to Emmaus, too, we are doing it alongside one another – whoever the 'other' happens to be. We are playing our part in the communion of saints, and that part is not optional if we proclaim ourselves Christians. We have responsibility to one another, because that is what being holy is all about.

So, in Lent, we are all called to become more fully

ourselves in communion with one another. This is no mere pie in the sky, imaginary state, but a real, lived out one, that has this-worldly consequences. This Lent, we are called to live in truthfulness with one another, to find our identity and belonging in our togetherness. For this reason, if for none other, our time in worship together is so important. Our need to worship God not only alone, in the quietness of our daily prayers, but together, in the noise and the challenge of the assembly of God, is real. In so doing, we become more and more like the prayerful community that God calls us into being – and we become more and more like ourselves.

Our calling is not insignificant: it is demanding. This is the way of God. Yet the way of God is also something that will never call us beyond what we can do and be, even if we sometimes feel stretched to breaking point. Our journeying this Lent is a journeying that will be tough at times, and yet it will be a journey where we will be accompanied by the God of the universe. Where we can, we are called to make time for God – with others, and in the silence of our hearts. Where we can, we are called to enable others to do the same. The 'where we can' matters, because this call is to help us become more truly ourselves, rather than less. Lent is a time to reset, but it is not a time to feel helplessly guilty about what we simply cannot achieve. Sometimes we do need a stern word to remind us that our priorities are askew. Sometimes we need a gentle whisper to remind us that we really are doing our best. We cannot change our beloved-ness to God – all we can do is sense it a little more clearly.

I hope you might be called into that journey in these

pages. See what you can do to give a little more time to God and to neighbour. See if you can set aside time to really live through and experience the remembrance of Holy Week. See what you can do to help others do the same. For God, that is quite probably enough.

Chapter 1
A Brief Introduction

The Psalms

THERE ARE MANY PARTS of the Christian tradition that manage to speak through time, and amongst them is surely the gift that is the Psalms. These remarkable verses have been sung, prayed over, prayed with, and found their way into so many different walks of life since long before the Christian faith came into being. Their ability to speak into the contemporary world in an equally vibrant and challenging way as they could into the world of several millennia ago is testament to their enduring power and the extraordinary inspiration of the original writer or writers. It is to the Psalms that I encourage you to turn this Lent, as a book of music that can still make our hearts soar, and yet which can accompany us through our darkest moments, too.

I grew up in the English choral tradition, so the Psalms hold a very particular place in my life's journey as a Christian. Even now, I can remember almost all the words off by heart – although there are occasional lapses, as we choristers only sang Matins on Sundays, and hence I can generally only properly remember those Psalms set for Evensong. It is one of Cranmer's gifts that in the Book of Common Prayer we are encouraged to go through the entire book of Psalms every month. When I was a choirboy, it was with a mixture of dread and excitement that we looked forward to the fifteenth evening of the month, where was set psalm seventy-eight – with seventy-three verses! The thing is, whilst you might think that over seventy verses of psalmody might feel just a little too much for an evening, the stories of the faith told in that psalm, and some of the choice wording, enthralled even the most tricky of choristers.

After making our way through the first sixty-five verses, there was always the two wonderful following verses to come:

> So the Lord awaked as one out of sleep: and like a giant refreshed with wine.
> He smote his enemies in the hinder parts: and put them to a perpetual shame.

You can imagine how well that went down with the youngsters in the choir – we may have looked like angels but were much more frequently up to no good than we would ever like to admit. Of course, the language used in the Book of Common Prayer's psalmody, which is based on Myles Coverdale's translation of the Bible from 1535 and his later Psalter, is not always an entirely accurate transliteration – yet there is a poetic beauty to it which has inspired worshippers for hundreds of years, and which in its beauty allows the Psalms to speak to us in a way that can still stir up the imagination and points to the original way these great prayers, petitions, frustrations, indictments even, would have reached the ears of their hearers and the mouths of their singers.

A Brief Introduction

It is for that reason that it is Coverdale's Psalter that we will meet in these pages. You may, of course, have your own preference for particular translations, and I would strongly encourage you to have a look at how different translators have engaged with these great songs – what their emphases are, what they felt the original author or authors were trying to get across, and why. We know, of course, that it is not only in choral worship that the words of the Psalms can become familiar to us – anyone whose prime engagement with the Christian musical tradition is worship songs and choruses will also find themselves with the words of the Psalms on their lips time after time. They find their way, too, into idiom and everyday language; they are found at moments of great national importance like the coronation (for example, the words of 'I was Glad' as the King entered Westminster Abbey); they shape much of our lives as Christians, or even just as cultural Christians, with the words of Psalm twenty-three – 'The Lord is my Shepherd' – frequently amongst the words sung in our last earthly journey.

The Psalms are, of course, biblical – in the Jewish and Christian traditions, we find one hundred and fifty of them in our Bibles, and in both traditions the Psalms have always and continue to form the backbone of our corporate worship. Their content is hugely varied and various – and sometimes rather shocking to those who have bought into the idea that all religions ever do is talk about 'being nice' to other people! You need only look at Psalm one hundred and thirty seven's final verses (which we politely omitted when we sang this particular psalm as choirboys) or the grotesqueness and anger of Psalm fifty-eight to realise that it is not only the positives of human experience that we find in these hymns.

How we handle some of the more unsavoury content is – like how we handle other parts of scripture which pose deep questions of meaning and appear anything but edifying (we might think, for example, of references to mass murders, to xenophobia, to slavery) – a point of contention, and different Christians will respond to the presence of these verses in different ways. As I have said above, we simply omitted the verses that seemed a bit much – others will be determined to keep them in as an exemplar of lived human experience, or out of concern not to do away with a jot or tittle of the word of God. These are not easy conversations, but they are important ones – and it may be that you find yourself quite challenged by verses you find in the Psalms in this book. What are we to do with verses which seem to suggest that God loves revenge or can be incited to hatred of our enemies? How, as Christians, do we read the Psalms through the lens of the Gospel? How might we learn a little more about the context in which these Psalms were first written? How might that help us to hear them aright in our own time?

The risk, as ever with biblical interpretation, is to receive the Psalms as something immutable and static, as though they are too hot to handle, and too dangerous to challenge. Such a response to the scriptures does us no favours – and it shows far too little respect to the words that God has given us for our learning and through which the Holy Spirit speaks. By singing the Psalms – singing hymns that others wrote – we find ourselves inhabiting something that not only has its genesis in the mind and experience of the biblical writers, but in words and ideas that have shaped worship of God for millennia. Our willingness, in a sense, not only to sing another's song, but to make it our own, and identify with it, is an extraordinarily powerful thing – and it should surely unsettle us.

Following Cranmer's plan of having set Psalms for each day can make this unsettling nature even more acute, because rather than choose a psalm that might speak to a particular occasion, or experience, or emotion – much like we have in this book – instead, we might find ourselves in a joyous mood singing about how 'I am a worm and no man'. So, too, we might find ourselves singing the great clamorous words of Psalm one hundred and fifty – O praise God in his holiness – when we are feeling rather miserable on the thirtieth evening of the month. The Psalms can help us engage with our emotions, certainly, yet they can help bring us out of our own cocoons, too. It is in grappling with them, being challenged by them and challenging them back, in finding within them such a rich tapestry of life, that we can begin to fully explore their richness. It is in digesting and inhabiting them that we might find ourselves swimming in a tide that brings us closer to the God we worship.

This is not a book of academic study – it does not seek to go into the 'controversy' as to whether King David really wrote the Psalms (most commentators would agree that he did not); the dating of individual Psalms; or even explore the complex conversations around what different Psalms are seeking to do or what their structure can tell us about their formation and meaning. We won't explore the extent to which there is an editorial plan for the Psalms as a whole; the meaning of 'selah'; or how precisely they fit into the worship in the Temple. We won't touch in much detail on the patristic writing on the Psalms or the way that their Jewishness has far too often been set aside – although we must surely pause to remember how antisemitism is so often rather too close for comfort in the way we read what we call the Old Testament. These are good and important questions, and if you are interested, I strongly encourage you to develop your understanding of the Psalms – learning is never a bad thing for a Christian!

In these pages, however, we will meet the Psalms as devotional texts – as texts to be prayed over, and to be prayed with, alongside. We will meet the Psalms as texts to be breathed in, and to be breathed out, too. We will meet the Psalms as music, as hymns and songs that perhaps call to our hearts first and our heads second. We will meet the Psalms as great poetry that can slow us down, and call us to reflect. We will meet the Psalms as individuals and together. We will meet the Psalms, too, as hymns and songs that point towards God – as worship. Ultimately, we will meet the Psalms as they meet us, and tarry a while with them.

I hope you will enjoy this brief glimpse into the richness of the Psalms and the worlds they speak from and into. For some, this might be the first time you've had the opportunity to use the Psalms in meditation on the days of Lent and the events of Holy Week – for others, I hope that your previous reflections and meditations might be enriched by revisiting this treasure trove. We will meet the stories of God's people in different times and different places. We will meet creation and redemption; we will meet the love of God and God's covenant with us; we will meet holiness, in all its varying forms, we will meet frustration at the ways of the world and find our own need for repentance, too. We will find ourselves looking towards the future of all things whilst not losing sight of the will and action of God in our present.

The Psalms in this book contain lament, protest, thanksgiving, and praise, wisdom and joy, trust and fear, history and future hope – and they are a mere taste of what a re-immersion in this most extraordinary of hymn books might do for us as Christians and as a church. 'Be filled with the Spirit, as you sing psalms and hymns and spiritual songs to one another, singing and making melody to the Lord in your hearts, giving thanks to God the Father at all times and for everything in the name of our Lord Jesus Christ', says St Paul (Ephesians 5:18b-20). Let us see where that might bring us on Easter morning.

This book

A number of Psalms will, then, form the lifeblood of this book – giving us a way to explore different scriptural passages, reflect on several themes, and travel through this great season. The format of the book is very simple – there is a chapter for each Sunday of Lent, together with chapters for Ash Wednesday, and for each day of Holy Week. We will finish our meditations on Easter Day, but there are plenty more Psalms to get stuck into during the Easter season if I have whetted your appetite!

Each chapter is structured in the same way – we first meet a psalm, then the Gospel reading allocated in the lectionary for the day (with very small alterations). There is then some material for reflection on the psalm and the reading, some pointers for prayer, and some questions which you might want to explore on your own or in a Lent group. The material is designed for both options: if you would like to explore with your church group, then you'll find prompters in each chapter; similarly, if you want to journey through Lent with this book as your accompanying guide then you'll be able to do that too. At the end of each chapter there is the Church of England's collect for the occasion – a prayer that gathers together the themes of the day and offers them to God.

The Gospel readings you'll find here are mostly from St Luke's Gospel – in the lectionary that the Church of England and many other churches use, each of the Synoptic Gospels gets a full airing every three years, and this year it is St Luke's turn. People often have their favourite Evangelist – St Luke 'the physician' seems particularly apposite for me. St Luke is known for his focus on the poor, the outcast, and for Gentile believers (he is thought to be writing as a Gentile to and for other Gentiles). St John takes centre stage during Holy Week, as happens each year, and we hear the words of St Matthew's Gospel on Ash Wednesday. You may find it interesting to do some comparing and contrasting of the way that different Evangelists tell the story of Christ's death and passion and think about what particularly jumps out to you from the pages – and of course next year you'll have the opportunity to walk this season with St Matthew.

The Gospel readings are primarily either events in the life, passion, and death of Jesus, or parables and lessons for Christian living told by Jesus to demonstrate something of the Kingdom that is ushered in with his death and resurrection. You will be drawn along through these moments to the very significant 'moments in time' of Holy Week – drawn on a journey through times and places. Yet you will be drawn, too, through a number of themes, themes which look to a world defined by peace through justice – a journey which culminates in the time, place, and theology of the Triduum (the three holy days starting on Maundy Thursday). Each chapter will include opportunities for you to reflect on yourself, on the church, and the world, and the things we might be being called to do and be this Lent. Be open to what you might learn from your own reflections – and those of other people. You might find yourself surprised.

If you can, I really encourage you to find a church to attend for Holy Week and try to do the lot. The experience of starting off in a Palm Sunday procession, then hearing the Gospel readings with their increasing tension, living through Jesus' last few days, the last supper, betrayal, agony in the garden, crucifixion, the emptiness of Holy Saturday, and then the joy of the resurrection, is an extraordinary and deeply rewarding time. You will not only feel more connected to the events of two thousand years ago – you will be, in some way, truly *there*. You will really go up to Jerusalem, albeit a Jerusalem that is partly in your mind and partly in your parish.

That might sound a bit over the top, even incredible, but Holy Week once properly experienced can call you back again and again. To experience the empty tomb without first experiencing the triumph, love, desolation and horror of Holy Week is to do yourself a disservice. This book is here as your guide, but no static words on a page can ever truly compete with experiencing with our bodies and our minds. If you decide to take something up for Lent, rather than give it up, then make it a full participation in this most holy of weeks.

Using this book

As I've said above, you might want to make use of this book as an individual, or in a church group. If the latter, you could have a session each week, and a daily session during Holy Week. You might want to read the chapters together, or read them before your sessions and use the time to engage with the questions and with wider conversation. You might want to base each of your sessions on the theme of the chapter, starting by reading the psalm together and hearing the words of the Gospel. Whichever way you choose to do it, make sure you take time to pray through the psalm – letting it soak into you. Take it home for a week, and maybe pray it each day, when you wake up in the morning and just before you go to bed. Let it do the work for you, and see it doing the work with those you meet with. What might it be saying to them in a different way to you? Why?

Of course, you may be making use of this as your own devotional book. You might be doing that as an old hand – Lent might be second nature to you, and if so, I hope you find new things to be excited about, and to fall in love with all over again. The stories of Holy Week are not only deeply profound but extraordinarily rich. The Psalms have so much to teach us, and give us words for things with which we might otherwise struggle. I pray you have a holy and invigorating time with them.

Finally, you might have read all of this and feel a bit confused – you might not really have much of a faith, but are approaching Lent for the first time, as an opportunity to take a step back and refocus your life. If that's you, please stick with it. Allow yourselves to experience something of the Christian faith in these pages, and hear a little bit about the man who Christians have spent millennia seeking to follow, however imperfectly. Hear some of the ancient hymns of the people of God. See where it might take you. You never know where you'll end up.

Chapter 2

Ash Wednesday: Preparation, Repentance, Reflection, and Sin

HAVE MERCY UPON ME, O God, after thy great goodness; according to the multitude of thy mercies do away mine offences.

Wash me throughly from my wickedness, and cleanse me from my sin.

For I acknowledge my faults, and my sin is ever before me.

Against thee only have I sinned, and done this evil in thy sight; that thou mightest be justified in thy saying, and clear when thou shalt judge.

Behold, I was shapen in wickedness, and in sin hath my mother conceived me.

But lo, thou requirest truth in the inward parts, and shalt make me to understand wisdom secretly.

Thou shalt purge me with hyssop, and I shall be clean; thou shalt wash me, and I shall be whiter than snow.

Thou shalt make me hear of joy and gladness, that the bones which thou hast broken may rejoice.

Turn thy face from my sins, and put out all my misdeeds.

Make me a clean heart, O God, and renew a right spirit within me.

Cast me not away from thy presence, and take not thy holy Spirit from me.

O give me the comfort of thy help again, and stablish me with thy free Spirit.

Then shall I teach thy ways unto the wicked, and sinners shall be converted unto thee.

Deliver me from blood-guiltiness, O God, thou that art the God of my health; and my tongue shall sing of thy righteousness.

Thou shalt open my lips, O Lord, and my mouth shall show thy praise.

For thou desirest no sacrifice, else would I give it thee; but thou delightest not in burnt-offerings.

The sacrifice of God is a troubled spirit: a broken and contrite heart, O God, shalt thou not despise.

O be favourable and gracious unto Sion; build thou the walls of Jerusalem.

Then shalt thou be pleased with the sacrifice of righteousness, with the burnt-offerings and oblations; then shall they offer young bullocks upon thine altar.

Psalm 51

Ash Wednesday

"Beware of practicing your righteousness before others in order to be seen by them, for then you have no reward from your Father in heaven.

"So whenever you give alms, do not sound a trumpet before you, as the hypocrites do in the synagogues and in the streets, so that they may be praised by others. Truly I tell you, they have received their reward. But when you give alms, do not let your left hand know what your right hand is doing, so that your alms may be done in secret, and your Father who sees in secret will reward you.

"And whenever you pray, do not be like the hypocrites, for they love to stand and pray in the synagogues and at the street corners, so that they may be seen by others. Truly I tell you, they have received their reward. But whenever you pray, go into your room and shut the door and pray to your Father who is in secret, and your Father who sees in secret will reward you.

"And whenever you fast, do not look sombre, like the hypocrites, for they mark their faces to show others that they are fasting. Truly I tell you, they have received their reward. But when you fast, put oil on your head and wash your face, so that your fasting may be seen not by others but by your Father who is in secret, and your Father who sees in secret will reward you.

"Do not store up for yourselves treasures on earth, where moth and rust consume and where thieves break in and steal, but store up for yourselves treasures in heaven, where neither moth nor rust consumes and where thieves do not break in and steal. For where your treasure is, there your heart will be also."

Matthew 6:1-6, 16-21

Lent gets a bit of a bad name. Whilst so much of contemporary Christianity seems desperate to emulate – even ape – those things that the world outside always does better (we might think of pop concerts, charismatic leaders, purity politics), this period of fasting, of repentance, this time when we dare whisper the word 'sin', feels a bit *too churchy*. We seem increasingly worried about being 'inaccessible', a word with little definition and so often even less meaning, and so we don't want to get caught up in all the sin talk, in all the hard, guilt-inducing stuff that appears to have bothered the medieval church rather less than that in our own time. Sin, and the need for repentance, is just a bit unattractive, a bit weird, a bit too miserable. It's not shiny enough.

Now Lent, of course, does not have to be all about sin – there are many other important things that we might think about and do during this season. During Lent we might quite rightly take some time out and spend more time reading the scriptures and reflecting on the mighty deeds of God. We might use it to try to become a little more like the people that God has called us to be. There are a whole host of things we might do, from the simpler (trying to attend Mass a little more often, trying to go to the gym a little more often!) to the more challenging (trying to find more time for charity or works of mercy, trying to find our colleagues just a tiny bit less irritating!). Yet one thing we really cannot do is have a good and holy Lent without engaging in reflection on sin and repentance.

Sin might be unpopular, it might be out of vogue, but in the depths of our hearts we know that it is very much here, and very much part of not only our individual lives but also our lives together. Sin permeates so much, whether we want to take responsibility for it or not. Sin lies in our broken relationships, in our ravaging God's good creation, in our failure to play our part in the dismantling of oppressive structures of society. Sin lies in our unwillingness to see the image of God in the other – the image which God has put there whether we like it or not. Sin lies in our dogged refusal to follow the commands of God – at their simplest, to love God and neighbour – and in our endless determination to choose the easy and dishonest over the difficult and decent. Sin sticks to us – it *clings* to us, as the phrase goes – and as much as we want to pretend that we live in a post-sin society, in a world that doesn't need such an outdated concept, we cannot get away from that reality. What we can choose to do is to pretend it isn't there – the problem is that this achieves precisely nothing, and merely makes matters worse.

You and I will have our own particular favourite sins, the ones we pretend don't really matter that much. You and I will have our own unconscious sins, too, sins that might be picked up by those who know us best, but which we cannot quite bring ourselves to accept belong to us. We're much better at pointing out other people's sins, too – to our minds, our own are always either less present or less serious. Our sins don't stay isolated – they become patterns of behaviour, ways of *being*. You are what you eat – in many ways, you are what you sin. Yes, our sin is often in the doing – but our sins go deeper than that. Sin is more than the sum of our sins – it is closer to a way of life, a web of dishonour that keeps us tangled within it.

It impacts on our life together – it spreads out from our own carefully curated existences into the wider world, and gets embedded, generation after generation, in the way our society works – in the way our society *is*. There are many ways of thinking about 'original sin', the idea that our behaviour errs towards the wrong and the sinful ever since the disobedience of Adam in the Garden of Eden. One way is surely to take a look at the world around us and see quite how much sin pervades society – 'structural sin'. Another is to look at how we so often choose the wrong thing in our own lives. Neither of these forms of sin is something we can merely ignore or blame on someone else. Both of them have a very real impact on who we are and how we are. As much as we like to pretend that we are automatous, we are nothing of the sort – we are ultimately relational, in a way that transcends time and space.

As we sin, we do damage not only to our relationships with God and with other people, to our *communion*, but we do damage to the image of God that we bear, too. That image becomes more marred, more imperfect, and in the process, we become less ourselves. Yet we remain wedded to our sins, because it's easier that way. We don't really fancy putting in the hard work that might help us escape from the cycle – and sometimes it's more than not fancying it. Like St Paul, writing in Romans 7, we do not do what we want, but the very thing we hate, and we do not understand our actions. Who will rescue us?

In today's Gospel reading, Jesus calls us to do some self-examination. There is much to be said for Jesus' emphasis on doing things in secret and not simply to be seen by others, but one of the most important things to take from Jesus' words is surely the innate importance of engaging in things like fasting, praying, and giving alms. In other words, Jesus is calling us to do these things for their own sake, rather than to be given early reward for seeming to do the *right thing*, something that remains just as relevant in the present day. Jesus calls us to do these things in the right way, because these things matter.

Fasting has long been associated with Lent, yet today's Gospel can make even our contemporary practices associated with this fasting feel a bit uncomfortable. Many of us will have been or will go to church today, and receive ash on our foreheads, with words to remind us that we are dust, and to dust we shall return. Many of us will then proudly wear that ash to work or to school, on the bus or to the supermarket. What exactly is our motivation for doing so? Of course, ash on our foreheads marks us out as disciples of Christ and might be a talking point that opens us up to questions about the faith we profess. Yet it is not entirely impossible for us to fall into the trap of this ashing being little more than an outward-facing, isolated piety – the kind of outward piety that Jesus warns us about when he tells us to put oil on our head and wash our face, so that our fasting may be seen not by others but by our Father.

Similarly, whilst we might feel more pious that we are giving up chocolate, or eating only fish on Fridays, if there is no purpose to that beyond a general feel-good factor, then it is hard to see what benefit is really being derived for our spiritual life. It is much easier to do the externals – the 'burnt-offerings' that God 'delightest not in', as the psalmist puts it – without engaging with the internals. Further, it is easy to engage with the internals if we do not dig too deep, or allow ourselves to really reflect on who and what we are, and how that accords with the person God has called us to be. It is hard to properly repent if we do not take the time to figure out the '*for what*'.

'But lo, thou requirest truth in the inward parts', says the psalmist. How often do we spend enough time to even scratch the surface of that truth? How much do we really want to go there – and how much are we willing to 'acknowledge our faults'? How often we would rather merely be cleansed and washed, without taking the time to find out which bits of us need a little more time and attention. How often we would rather jump to the end of the psalm rather than start from the beginning and do the hard work of acknowledging reality.

All is not, of course, doom and gloom. All is not lost. One of the extraordinary claims of the Christian faith is that despite everything, we really are forgiven. We really are forgiven not because we have done anything, but because God has. We really are forgiven because of the events we look forward to in Holy Week, and that we are called to begin our period of preparation for today. We really are forgiven.

If we really are forgiven, then that might call us to do two things. The first of those is to act like you or I really are forgiven, like we believe it. That's not the same as suggesting that anything goes – forgiveness doesn't come like cheap grace, and acting like we are forgiven means we must be more, and not less, committed to searching out our inward parts. If our forgiveness is real, and good, and holy, if we really believe it to be so, then we cannot at the same time continue to try to hide things from the God who forgives. Being entirely forgiven demands offering our entire selves – allowing God to make us a clean heart, and renew our spirit.

The second thing our being forgiven might demand of us is to act like *we* really are forgiven – that is, you and me both, and all the rest of them too. 'Forgive us our trespasses, *as we forgive them that trespass against us*'. If our forgiveness is utterly unearned, utterly free, then the bad news, for those of us who like to hold a grudge, is that others' forgiveness is utterly unearned, and utterly free, too. Our own forgiveness calls us to find a way to live in a world in which that forgiven-ness is real for everyone, and not only for the deserving few – of which we might, surprisingly, feel that we are one.

Of course, living in a world marked by forgiven-ness does not mean that we have to suddenly blot out the past, or find ourselves blamed for not 'finding it in our hearts' to forgive others who have done us or others terrible wrongs. Sometimes, it really is too hard – sometimes, it really is not healthy – and sometimes, it really, *really* is not the place of the church to demand forgiveness. We can all probably remember times when we have seen the remarkable grace of forgiveness work its way into lives that have been so damaged, so hurt by others, and yet lives which are immeasurably graced by the opportunity to speak words of forgiveness. Such opportunities do come around, and in those moments a glimpse of the God who forgives is surely seen. Yet as is so often the case in matters of Christian ethics and wider Christian living, it is not for us to demand something of others – it is for us to ask ourselves how we might live lives graced by forgiveness.

For some of us, that really will mean letting go of old grudges against people, which serve no purpose except to continue to drag us down and make us angry and bitter. Sometimes that letting go will need us to seek professional help – not because we've done something wrong, but because the wrong done to us has a hold over us that we need to be freed from. For some of us, it will mean finding ways to help others, turning our own hurt into a spur for changing others' lives for the better. For some of us, it will mean finding a way to bear our grief and anger in a way that damages us the least. Yet for all of us, it means finding a deep solidarity, recognising our life is social and connected, and where one amongst us is hurting or suffering, then we all have a responsibility to play our part in the healing.

What we definitely can say, then, about forgiveness, and repentance, is that it is no static process. Repentance requires us not only to turn to God, but to turn to ourselves, too, and do the hard work of reflection. Repentance means being open to being purged with hyssop, not as punishment, but in the same way that shining a light in a darkened room can sometimes have the unfortunate consequence of us seeing things we'd rather not see. Repentance may indeed give us a 'troubled spirit' – it may give us a 'broken and a contrite heart' – but it is only through being honest with ourselves that we can ever truly find ourselves open to the multitude of God's mercies that can do away our offences. It is that multitude of mercies that is offered to you and me, us together, if we are willing to open our whole selves up to its balm.

So today, as we enter Lent, let us begin that process of deep inner reflection. Let us pause a moment to ask ourselves what parts of our lives we would simply rather not deal with – that we would rather God simply pretended weren't there. Let us truly believe in the comfort of the help of God – the possibility of a renewal of a right spirit. Let us begin to offer the sacrifice of righteousness – the offering of our whole lives to the God who has already forgiven us.

It is time, dear friends, to prepare ourselves once again for the possibility of grace.

Questions for discussion

• How do you plan to prepare this Lent?

• Does the idea of sin make sense to you or make you feel uncomfortable? Why do you think that might be?

• What does 'sin' mean to you? What kind of things does it bring to mind?

• What might your 'favourite' sins be? What might your motivation be for minimising their importance?

• What sins do you think your nearest and dearest might identify in you, if you let them?

- What is the place of repentance in your life?

- What are the things that stop you opening up your whole self for forgiveness?

- Do you truly think of yourself as forgiven – or even forgivable?

Prayer

Almighty and everlasting God,
you hate nothing that you have made
and forgive the sins of all those who are penitent:
create and make in us new and contrite hearts
that we, worthily lamenting our sins
and acknowledging our wretchedness,
may receive from you, the God of all mercy,
perfect remission and forgiveness;
through Jesus Christ your Son our Lord,
who is alive and reigns with you,
in the unity of the Holy Spirit,
one God, now and for ever.

Chapter 3

The First Sunday of Lent: Reliance

WHOSO DWELLETH UNDER THE defence of the Most High, shall abide under the shadow of the Almighty.

I will say unto the LORD, Thou art my hope, and my stronghold; my God, in him will I trust.

For he shall deliver thee from the snare of the hunter, and from the noisome pestilence.

He shall defend thee under his wings, and thou shalt be safe under his feathers; his faithfulness and truth shall be thy shield and buckler.

Thou shalt not be afraid for any terror by night, nor for the arrow that flieth by day;

For the pestilence that walketh in darkness, nor for the sickness that destroyeth in the noon-day.

A thousand shall fall beside thee, and ten thousand at thy right hand; but it shall not come nigh thee.

Yea, with thine eyes shalt thou behold, and see the reward of the ungodly.

For thou, LORD, art my hope; thou hast set

thine house of defence very high.
Here shall no evil happen unto thee, neither
shall any plague come nigh thy dwelling.
For he shall give his angels charge over thee, to
keep thee in all thy ways.
They shall bear thee in their hands, that thou
hurt not thy foot against a stone.
Thou shalt go upon the lion and adder: the
young lion and the dragon shalt thou tread
under thy feet.
Because he hath set his love upon me, therefore
will I deliver him; I will set him up, because he
hath known my Name.
He shall call upon me, and I will hear him; yea,
I am with him in trouble; I will deliver him, and
bring him to honour.
With long life will I satisfy him, and show him
my salvation.

Psalm 91

Jesus, full of the Holy Spirit, returned from the Jordan and was led by the Spirit in the wilderness, where for forty days he was tested by the devil. He ate nothing at all during those days, and when they were over he was famished. The devil said to him, "If you are the Son of God, command this stone to become a loaf of bread." Jesus answered him, "It is written, 'One does not live by bread alone.' "

Then the devil led him up and showed him in an instant all the kingdoms of the world. And the devil said to him, "To you I will give all this authority and their glory, for it has been given over to me, and I give it to anyone I please. If you, then, will worship me, it will all be yours." Jesus answered him, "It is written,

'Worship the Lord your God,and serve only him.' "

Then the devil led him to Jerusalem and placed him on the pinnacle of the temple and said to him, "If you are the Son of God, throw yourself down from here, for it is written,

'He will command his angels concerning you, to protect you,'

and

'On their hands they will bear you up, so that you will not dash your foot against a stone.' "

Jesus answered him, "It is said, 'Do not put the Lord your God to the test.' " When the devil had finished every test, he departed from him until an opportune time.

Luke 4:1-13

If one thing can be said about humankind, it is that we are extremely adept at telling ourselves lies – and believing them. Sometimes we know we're doing it, and yet we still believe them – at other times, we buy into the untruths of others, and end up creating false worlds around us where truth and lie are indistinguishable. Sometimes the lies we tell ourselves are self-referential; sometimes they are told in self-defence; sometimes they are merely convenient. We have seen the power of believing what we want to believe, or what is convenient, a number of times in recent years, with 'fake news' becoming increasingly difficult to distinguish from real events, and where the marketplace for ideology has started to impinge on what would previously have been held to be factual.

As much as we might not like to admit it, we are all prone to these strange beliefs – it is an inescapable part of contemporary living. However much we might voice our howls of outrage, we know that none of us is immune from the suggestive comment or the selective interpretation. Sometimes it is innocuous – sometimes, rather less so. Sometimes we know that what we're peddling is not quite true – yet we peddle it nonetheless. All the while we can deceive ourselves by denying the impact these little lies might have on ourselves, others, or our relationships with them. 'It's free speech', we might say, whilst apparently forgetting that as people of faith, nothing we say or do can ever be entirely 'free', at least in the way that the world sees it.

As Christians, we are in some way bound – bound not in a way that diminishes us, but in a way that increases us, that makes us more ourselves. In finding our freedom in God, we are bound to ways of being and living that enable that freedom to be truly embedded in our lives. Sometimes those ways of being are tricky, and just occasionally it might feel that we are being denied the good stuff. Yet our being bound to God allows us to be more truly ourselves because it allows us to escape one of the biggest lies that we tell ourselves – that we are autonomous individuals. It allows us to find our identity not in ourselves, but in relationship – in being part of something bigger than ourselves, being both beloved children of God and being connected to one another.

This being connected matters, because it means we cannot merely shake off our responsibility to each other – Christians don't get that free pass.

So, any 'freedom' in the free speech, or the free action, or the free anything of Christians is freedom as defined by God and not by humankind. In other words, our freedom is not something which comes responsibility-free – it comes steeped in service, in our love of God and our love of others. A supposed 'freedom' that ultimately leaves us harming and diminishing others is no freedom at all, however convenient it might be for us. A 'freedom' that starts and ends with us is really just another way of worshipping the self – and in so doing, denying our utter reliance on God and our interconnectedness with others. The problem is, that's always been a temptation we are rather prone to.

It's this temptation to believing in our autonomy, to believing in that rather beguiling idea of being 'self-reliant', that our Gospel speaks to today. On the surface, this kind of idea has its attractions. We need only think of the horror that so often accompanies the idea of getting old, of needing to rely on others, of no longer being in control, to realise quite what a hold the idea of self-reliance still has on us. When Jesus speaks to Peter about the kind of death 'by which he would glorify God' in verses 18-19 of St John's Gospel, he describes it in this way: 'Very truly, I tell you, when you were younger, you used to fasten your own belt and to go wherever you wished. But when you grow old, you will stretch out your hands, and someone else will fasten a belt around you and take you where you do not wish to go.' The Gospel tells us that this refers to Peter's crucifixion, yet it surely speaks, too, to our fear of being reliant on others – to our no longer being able to determine where we go, dependent on the whims of others.

It's a particularly Western way of thinking about old age, perhaps, and in our increasingly atomised society, it is an understandable one. As a society, we frequently shut our elderly away, scared that they might remind us of our own mortality and show up the lies we tell ourselves about eternal youth. In doing so, we contribute to the idea that human beings can be a 'burden' – that they might, in some cases, be better off not here any longer. Arguments and debates around assisted dying continue to swirl, but we can surely all agree that people feeling that by simply being alive they are placing an unbearable burden on others is a serious indictment on where we find ourselves. We can – and must – do better than that.

It is interesting that in St Luke's telling of the temptations in the wilderness, Jesus has already spent forty days fasting by the time the devil shows up. The first thing we might note is Jesus being described as 'full of the Holy Spirit'. Luke uses this kind of phrase a number of times during the Gospels, and each time something about who Jesus is – his identity – is revealed. The temptations in the wilderness are no exception, and in his rather predictable questioning, it is Jesus' identity that he tries to provoke Him to deny, in a number of ways. In refusing to be bowed by this tiresome temptation, Jesus tells us about himself, about God, and about us, and does so in a way that shows exactly what the devil is up to – then, and now.

The devil goes about his pointless exercise in three ways – first, encouraging Jesus to perform an act of power, yet an act of power, magic even, that will satisfy only himself. Second, the devil tries to get Jesus to deny his reliance on God the Father, and grasp the power instead – an illusion, of course, since in doing so Jesus would have merely shown himself enthralled to the devil rather than the Father. Finally, the devil becomes that small voice that sneakily suggests 'But do you *really* believe God will look after you?'. Jesus takes no prisoners in his answers, and does so by refusing to allow the devil to succeed in his determination to misuse scripture. Good try – but no thanks.

Of course, for Jesus, all the things in the world – all the things that ever have been and ever will be – are indeed rightfully his, and yet still he refuses to misuse this. Yet in his response to the devil, he submits to the Father – he declares himself needful of this relationship, obedient and holy. Unlike Adam in the Garden of Eden, Jesus does not take an inward turn, ready to declare himself to have no need of God. Instead, despite being the Son of God, he emphasises his reliance, his connectedness, his distinct *lack* of autonomy. His identity is relational – his identity is found not in self-reliance, but in love, which needs subject and object.

It is fascinating that, right at the start of Jesus' public ministry, we find these temptations. It is almost as though Jesus must first prove to himself, when nobody else is looking, who and what he is, before he is able to tell the rest of the world. His lack of sinfulness is not, sadly, something we can hope to emulate in its entirety, but his openness to the Holy Spirit and his clear willingness to have an integrity between his public and private life identity and self-understanding is something that can speak into our own lives as Christians. It's tempting for us to be self-effacing in public, to do and say the right thing when people are looking, but at the same time to be puffed up and pompous, and to do what we fancy rather than what we know we ought, when we are in the hiddenness of our own company. We see this human behaviour time and time again – we might think of various expenses scandals, of the public hateful prejudice and the private dalliances of various different figures in public life, or of the temptation that lies in all of us that we might 'get away with it' when we think nobody is looking. It's easy to point fingers at those who do this all too publicly – but let's not pretend we don't do it, too.

Another notable thing is the way the devil misuses scripture by making it his plaything, his tool. In all our debates about scripture in recent years, it is far too easy – wherever we end up in our answers to the endless debates that encircle our churches – to see scripture as primarily something to *use* rather than something to inhabit, to live within and from, and which speaks *to* us. Using scripture – and all too often using our faith in its entirety – in this way is to do it a serious disservice, and in many ways it is yet another way of declaring ourselves self-reliant, where scripture is given to us to make our point rather than as the word of God. That's not to say that we cannot ask questions of scripture – quite the opposite – but it is to say that we must always be alert to our listening to it with a filter on, determined to hear what we want it to say, what might be most convenient, or what might merely back up what we already thought.

The way today's psalm is used by the devil is a key example of this. 'They shall bear thee in their hands, that thou hurt not thy foot against a stone' is not, as the devil is trying to suggest, an isolated verse that can be used as a weapon, or as a tool of self-aggrandisement, or as something to be used to demand what we want, when we want it, from God. Read as a whole, today's psalm is most clearly a call to abide, to dwell – to rely on God. 'Because he hath set his love upon me', we are told, then God will hear us and deliver us – and because we are willing to be reliant on God, then the terror by night, the arrow by day, the pestilence that walketh in darkness, the sickness that destroyeth in the noon-day, none of these holds power over us. We can only be delivered from the snare of the hunter if we are willing to say that we need to be delivered – that God is our hope and our stronghold. We can only be reliant, if, like the psalmist, we can say 'my God, in him will I trust'.

It is in this reliance, borne through trust, that we might then begin to re-find our own identity. It is God who created us, without our help; who redeemed us, despite our never-ending rebellion; who sustains us, filling us with the Holy Spirit and gracing the world. In other words, we are utterly reliant on God whether we like it or not, whether we like to admit it or not. Our entire self is gifted to us, and we have done nothing whatsoever to deserve it or win it. Yet it is still gifted.

A recognition of and living into that free giftedness demands an awful lot of us – it demands that we not only know ourselves reliant, but that we act like it, too. It demands that we stop pretending that we are autonomous or atomised, that we have no need of God or of one another. It demands that we live our lives in a way that shines out in practical ways our recognising the giftedness not only of our own lives but of others' too. It calls us into communion with one another, a communion of fellowship and love that first speaks of *we* and *us* rather than *me* or *I*. That's not the same as saying we as individuals do not matter – but it is saying that our individuality is most truly found in communion with others.

It is in our relating – in our loving – that we are most fully ourselves. That relating starts with God – and our reliance on the God of the universe points to our need to recognise and even dare to embrace our reliance on other people, and them on us. We might then find not only our reliance on one another, but begin to rediscover our place within the entire created order, taking account once again of our need to take care – to steward – those things freely given to *us*, and not merely given to you or me.

Whoso dwelleth under the defence of the Most High, shall abide under the shadow of the Almighty. This is a promise, and not a threat – something to rejoice in, and not something to fear. It will take some courage to let go of our sense of self-sufficiency, certainly, but that sense is false in any case. We are not reliant on God because we say so – we are reliant on God because that is what reality looks like. It's learning to live a little more into that reality which is our task this Lent.

Questions for discussion

- How does being reliant on others make you feel? Why might you feel that way?

- What does freedom look like in your life?

- What do you think contemporary society might do differently to embrace rather than reject reliance?

- Which of the temptations would you have feared the most? Why?

- How might you become increasingly the same person in public and in private? How comfortable do you feel when it is just God and you in the room?

- What examples of giftedness can you identify in your own life's journey?

- How does today's psalm's message speak to you?

- What might being 'full of the Holy Spirit' look like in your life and in the lives of those around you?

Prayer

Almighty God,
whose Son Jesus Christ fasted forty days
in the wilderness,
and was tempted as we are, yet without sin:
give us grace to discipline ourselves in obedience
to your Spirit;
and, as you know our weakness,
so may we know your power to save;
through Jesus Christ your Son our Lord,
who is alive and reigns with you,
in the unity of the Holy Spirit,
one God, now and for ever.

Chapter 4

The Second Sunday of Lent: Lament

HEAR MY PRAYER, O LORD, and let my
crying come unto thee.
Hide not thy face from me in the time of my
trouble; incline thine ear unto me when I call;
O hear me, and that right soon.
For my days are consumed away like smoke,
and my bones are burnt up as it were
a firebrand.
My heart is smitten down, and withered like
grass; so that I forget to eat my bread.
For the voice of my groaning, my bones will
scarce cleave to my flesh.
I am become like a pelican in the wilderness,
and like an owl that is in the desert.
I have watched, and am even as it were a
sparrow, that sitteth alone upon the housetop.
Mine enemies revile me all the day long; and
they that are mad upon me are sworn
together against me.
For I have eaten ashes as it were bread, and

mingled my drink with weeping;
And that, because of thine indignation and
wrath; for thou hast taken me up, and cast me
down.
My days are gone like a shadow, and I am
withered like grass.
But thou, O LORD, shalt endure for ever, and
thy remembrance throughout all generations.
Thou shalt arise, and have mercy upon Sion; for
it is time that thou have mercy upon her, yea,
the time is come.
And why? Thy servants think upon her stones,
and it pitieth them to see her in the dust.
The nations shall fear thy Name, O LORD; and
all the kings of the earth thy majesty;
When the LORD shall build up Sion, and when
his glory shall appear;
When he turneth him unto the prayer of the
poor destitute, and despiseth not their desire.
This shall be written for those that come after,
and the people which shall be born shall praise
the LORD.
For he hath looked down from his sanctuary;
out of the heaven did the LORD behold the
earth;
That he might hear the mournings of such
as are in captivity, and deliver them that are
appointed unto death;
That they may declare the Name of the LORD
in Sion, and his worship at Jerusalem;
When the peoples are gathered together, and
the kingdoms also, to serve the LORD.

He brought down my strength in my journey,
and shortened my days.
But I said, O my God, take me not away in the
midst of mine age; as for thy years, they endure
throughout all generations.
Thou, Lord, in the beginning hast laid the
foundation of the earth, and the heavens are the
work of thy hands.
They shall perish, but thou shalt endure: they
all shall wax old as doth a garment;
And as a vesture shalt thou change them, and
they shall be changed; but thou art the same,
and thy years shall not fail.
The children of thy servants shall continue, and
their seed shall stand fast in thy sight.

Psalm 102

At that very hour some Pharisees came and said to him, 'Get away from here, for Herod wants to kill you.' He said to them, 'Go and tell that fox for me, "Listen, I am casting out demons and performing cures today and tomorrow, and on the third day I finish my work. Yet today, tomorrow, and the next day I must be on my way, because it is impossible for a prophet to be killed outside of Jerusalem." Jerusalem, Jerusalem, the city that kills the prophets and stones those who are sent to it! How often have I desired to gather your children together as a hen gathers her brood under her wings, and you were not willing! See, your house is left to you. And I tell you,

you will not see me until the time comes when you say, "Blessed is the one who comes in the name of the Lord.'"

Luke 13:31-35

There are a number of haunting phrases that the Gospel writers include in their narratives. Today's Gospel certainly contains one of those – 'see, your house is left to you'. We see Jesus experiencing a number of emotions during his life, ministry, and passion, and today we see Him lament. You could read Jesus' words here in a number of different ways – frustration, anger even, but I wonder whether Jesus is really simply exhaling and looking with the mixture of disappointment, sadness, powerlessness, and dread that is so often found in biblical lament. 'How often have I desired to gather your children together as a hen gathers her brood under her wings, and you were not willing', says Jesus, reminiscent of another scene in St Matthew's Gospel (Matthew 11:16-19). There, Jesus' lament comes as the people criticise both him and John the Baptist for their various forms of ministry – Jesus for being 'a glutton and a drunkard, a friend of tax collectors and sinners', and John for having 'a demon'. 'Yet wisdom is vindicated by her deeds', says Jesus. In those evocative words, you can almost hear the tired grief in his voice.

Lament is not a million miles away from despair, yet there is a distinct difference – lament has a purpose. In the world of today, it is so easy to fall into despair. Those things that have always marred human life continue to press in on every side, with lessons unlearnt and warnings unheeded.

Global conflicts, wars, natural disasters, civil unrest – all continue, with no apparent let up. We continue to destroy and defile not only our fellow humanity, but the natural world, too. The very human desires for power and control lead to never-ending examples of greed, violence, and degradation. Envy and lust are never far beneath the surface either. Nothing is really new under the sun – we humans are far too good at reheating and repackaging our historical wrongdoings to bother inventing anything new. Looking out at it all, it is hard not to be at least a little disheartened, even if we are the world's top optimist.

Yet the way of God does not call us to despair, although nor does it call us to pretend all is well. We live in a world redeemed by God, however much that can be hard to believe at times. We live lives that have themselves been redeemed, in a community of the redeemed. It is through faith that we realise that hope, and it is through love that we put it into action, yet our own feeble attempts to make things better – to participate in the re-creative will of God – can sometimes feel just too little to make any difference. Yet still, it is not to despair that we are called, but hope. Bearing witness to that hope may well require us to lament.

Lament is not a rare occurrence in the Bible, and speaks perhaps of the broken-heartedness that lies deep within God, when God looks upon the world and the continued mess we make of it. Lament, too, speaks to the response of many holy men and women when faced with human evil, or human wilfulness, or simply human disregard. 'Go and tell that fox for me', says Jesus, and there is flash of anger here, 'listen, I am casting out demons and performing cures today and tomorrow, and on the third day I finish my work'. Jesus is, of course, pointing towards the summit of his passion in Jerusalem, yet there is a wry humour underlying this anger, too. You also find this elsewhere in the Gospels – Jesus is said to be unable to do any great works of power, so merely heals a few of the sick, as though that is a mere trifling matter! Herod – you might want to kill me, but in the meantime I will cast out some demons and cure some folk, and then you can come after me! There is a humour and an anger here, but there is a resistance, too, and that resistance sits at the heart of lament. It is in the clothes of resistance that hope takes its rightful place.

Resistance and solidarity have long been important parts of human struggle, yet we are not always comfortable with them in our ecclesial life. There is an air of struggle, of uneasiness, even of embarrassment, in the idea of resistance and solidarity, and for a long time the church has appeared rather unwilling to go there. We might think of the extraordinary turnaround in the Roman Catholic Church in recent years, where opposition to the ideas underlying liberation theology from South America has yielded to Pope Francis's call (himself not always at ease with such ideas) for a poor church for the poor. The church is always something of a tanker in the time it takes to turn around, but it does feel that perhaps we are finally learning to listen to the words of Jesus that call us to the margins, not merely to bring them into the centre, but to dwell there a while. Solidarity with the oppressed, and resistance to the oppressing forces, and even the oppressors, can be a tricky game for a church far too used to social propriety and that frequently stands on its own dignity, yet it is what the Lord calls us to do.

The Second Sunday of Lent

Up goes the cry, of course, that the church should keep its nose out of politics. Stick to the pulpit, Father, as someone once said to me after I'd dared to mention the violence being disproportionately meted out to Black people on the streets of London. The thing is, that *is* the pulpit, or at least it is part of it. Priests are not called to be social workers, but we are called to name and proclaim everything in the light of the Gospel of Jesus Christ. Similarly, Christians aren't called to belong to any particular political party, but we are forbidden from neatly separating out our church life and our day to day. If we choose not to name things, or choose not to do things, out of fear that by doing or naming things we will be labelled as political, then we are acting politically, nonetheless. Our omissions matter. Similarly, a refusal to stand alongside the oppressed and to cosset ourselves in our own fantasy world in which we merely put our fingers in our ears when we hear something that should call us to action is not the Christian way. That is not what being a good and faithful servant is all about.

Yet even if we do show resistance, and even if we do sometimes find ways to show that solidarity, nonetheless things can still feel too much to bear. That might be dismay at the ways of the world, or it might be despondency when meditating upon our own lives. Like the psalmist, we might feel our bones scarcely cleaving to our flesh, our heart smitten down and our days consumed away like smoke. Those extraordinary images portray with such beauty how it might feel – I am become like a pelican in the wilderness and like an owl that is in the desert; I have watched, and am even as it were a sparrow, that sitteth alone upon the housetop. There are times where our mere carrying on feels too much to bear – where, like Jesus, we might look out to Jerusalem and sigh with sighs too deep for words as the Spirit intercedes for us.

Of course, in recent years Jerusalem itself remains a place over which great sorrow must surely be felt. A city that so many, of so many different religious groups, call holy and the mount of God, has been a battle ground for millennia. In our own day, so it continues. Yet we might look, too, to the Jerusalem of our hearts – to the place which we call holy and a gateway to heaven, and yet in our own hearts that place is often torn apart by grief and sorrow, frustration and anger, hopelessness and despair. How many broken and unhealed relationships we carry in our hearts; how many hard and painful things, whilst all the time our hearts become battlegrounds for competing interests and human desire. In the process, how little we find God there.

Yet, whilst Jesus laments, he points, too, to the future that God has in store. There will be a time when Jerusalem will say 'blessed is the one who comes in the name of the Lord'. There will be a time when things are different, because there will be a time when God's purposes are worked out and where God's sovereignty will be revealed. There will, someday, be such a time.

The Psalms of lament, of which there are a number, take a similar course. For whilst we are indeed given words to name our sorrow and our grief, our anger and our frustration, words which can sometimes feel uncomfortable in their rawness, nonetheless these Psalms do not allow despair to have the last word. In today's psalm, we can see the pivot at verse twelve – the 'but', which changes everything. Yet that 'but' does not change things by pretending away the first eleven verses, or by demanding that we pretend all is well when it is not. Nor does it neatly separate the 'now' from some imagined (or even imaginary) future, where if only we were a little more optimistic, we might find some good news. Instead, the psalmist calls us to a recognition that despite the very real and concrete, and not imagined, present difficulties, nonetheless there is something about the nature of God which transcends these, and which is having an impact here and now, even if we cannot recognise it. 'For he hath looked down from his sanctuary; out of the heaven did the Lord behold the earth – this shall be written for those that come after, and the people which shall be born shall praise the Lord'.

The psalmist, in the midst of despair, is able to hope in the solidarity of God with God's people. This solidarity is no vain hope, but a real and concrete thing, just as real and concrete as the circumstances that have sent the psalmist into sorrow and grief. This solidarity is a thing of trust – a thing promised, promised despite the unworthiness of those to whom it is promised. Even when the psalmist feels the need to implore God, to ask that the crying comes unto God and that God might incline God's ear right soon, nonetheless such a request is made *because* of the implicit trust that the psalmist has in the God who *will* do such a thing. The God of the Bible, the God of Jesus Christ, is a God who does hear, who does endure for ever, who does not despise the desire of the poor destitute or turn away from the mournings of such as are in captivity, who makes 'the children of thy servants' to continue, and 'their seed [to] stand fast in thy sight'.

That is the creative tension we are called to find ways to embody in our lives as Christians, and to vicariously hold on behalf of the world. There is a changelessness to God and a changefulness to humanity, and our journey towards God is not one in which we are told to ignore the facts of human sin and depravity (ours included) in front of our eyes, but nor is it one in which those facts are permitted to be anything like the reality that is God. God *is*: I am who I am – thus you shall say to the Israelites, 'I am has sent me to you' (Exodus 3:14). God's presence and God's God-ness is more real than anything in the world, not because it somehow magics the pain and sorrow into nothing, but because, standing as the ultimate redemptive reality, the world has already been transformed. God's being God remains, whilst everything else is fleeting. 'They shall perish, but thou shalt endure: they all shall wax old as doth a garment'. Yet in Jesus Christ, that garment is one that God calls to Godself and redeems.

That garment is you and me, and the whole created order. That redemption has already been accomplished in the events we are preparing to celebrate once again this Lent. We are called to lament – and in our lament, we are called to speak those words of resistance: God *is*.

Questions for discussion

- What particularly grieves you about the world of today?

- How do we hold on to the reality of God's 'God-ness' whilst still honouring lived realities of pain and grief?

- What is the place of anger in the Christian life?

- Have ideas of solidarity and resistance formed part of your Christian journey? Why? How?

- How does the metaphor that Jesus uses of a hen and her chicks strike you? Does it surprise you?

- How might 'our house being left to us' apply to situations in our own lives?

- Where might the Psalms of lament have a role in your spiritual life?

Prayer

Almighty God,
you show to those who are in error the light
of your truth,
that they may return to the way of righteousness:
grant to all those who are admitted
into the fellowship of Christ's religion,
that they may reject those things
that are contrary to their profession,
and follow all such things as are agreeable to the same;
through our Lord Jesus Christ,
who is alive and reigns with you,
in the unity of the Holy Spirit,
one God, now and for ever.

Chapter 5

The Third Sunday of Lent: Sanctification

BLESSED IS HE WHOSE
unrighteousness is forgiven, and whose sin is
covered.
Blessed is the man unto whom the LORD
imputeth no sin, and in whose spirit
there is no guile.
For whilst I held my tongue, my bones
consumed away through my daily complaining.
For thy hand was heavy upon me day and
night, and my moisture was like the
drought in summer.
I acknowledged my sin unto thee; and mine
unrighteousness have I not hid.
I said, I will confess my sins unto the
LORD; and so thou forgavest the wickedness
of my sin.
For this shall every one that is godly make
his prayer unto thee, in a time when thou
mayest be found; surely the great water-floods
shall not come nigh him.

Thou art a place to hide me in; thou shalt preserve me from trouble; thou shalt compass me about with songs of deliverance.

I will inform thee, and teach thee in the way wherein thou shalt go; and I will guide thee with mine eye.

Be ye not like to horse and mule, which have no understanding; whose mouths must be held with bit and bridle, else they will not obey thee.

Great plagues remain for the ungodly; but whoso putteth his trust in the LORD, mercy embraceth him on every side.

Be glad, O ye righteous, and rejoice in the LORD; and be joyful, all ye that are true of heart.

Psalm 32

At that very time there were some present who told Jesus about the Galileans whose blood Pilate had mingled with their sacrifices. He asked them, 'Do you think that because these Galileans suffered in this way they were worse sinners than all other Galileans? No, I tell you, but unless you repent you will all perish as they did. Or those eighteen who were killed when the tower of Siloam fell on them—do you think that they were worse offenders than all the other people living in Jerusalem? No, I tell you, but unless you repent you will all perish just as they did.'

Then he told this parable: 'A man had a fig tree planted in his vineyard, and he came looking for fruit on it and found none. So he said to the man working the vineyard, "See here! For three years I have come looking for fruit on this fig tree, and still I find none. Cut it down! Why should it be wasting the soil?" He replied, "Sir, let it alone for one more year, until I dig around it and put manure on it. If it bears fruit next year, well and good, but if not, you can cut it down".'

Luke 13:1-9

What does it mean to be holy? Or, perhaps more importantly, what does it mean to *become* holy?

Most of us, even the most pious of us, would probably shrink a little at the idea of calling ourselves 'holy'. When I wrote *Queer Holiness*, a lot of people – particularly those with differing views to mine on LGBTQIA affirmation – told me that those two things really didn't go together. How can you be 'queer' and 'holy'? – it just didn't make sense to them. But sometimes, in deeper conversation, it would become clear to us that they didn't just find the idea of queerness being holy difficult (though they certainly did) – they found the whole idea of calling anything that might be seen as a human identity marker 'holy' fundamentally unacceptable. Only God is holy, only godly things are holy, went the argument. The holiness of the holy becomes sullied the moment it becomes too human.

Of course, there's some sense to that – for it is from

God that we get our fundamental identity, and it is in the light of our relationship to God that we derive whatever holiness we might have. Being holy means being dedicated, set aside, consecrated to God and godly things. We may never be fully holy, but it is our relationship to God, our orientation to God, that does the 'setting apart' that is necessary for any part of us to be called holy. Any human identity markers are ultimately subsumed in our identity in Christ, and it is that identity that gives us a glimpse of holiness.

Except I'm not sure that's quite the whole story. Our human identity markers, those things that set us apart in our life here on earth, are certainly not the be all and end all, and they are certainly taken up into our identity in Christ. Yet that being 'taken up' is not quite the same as being obliterated – our finding our identity in Christ means our whole selves finding our identity in Christ, and to do so, it's not at all clear that those things that mark us out here and now are cancelled or destroyed. This is by no means simple, of course – there is a process of discernment here, a way of trying to work out how our human identities contribute to our development as people and the way we engage with the wider world, and how the wider world engages with us.

I think there is good biblical precedent for this. Let's consider another of Jesus' parables described by Luke, that of the Rich Man and Lazarus (Luke 16:19-end). In this parable, it really matters what characteristics, what identity someone had in life, not because of it granting that person some kind of innate sense of self in the hereafter, but because of the relationships that such people developed and the impact that had on their engagement with the world. The richness of the rich man, who interestingly has no name, surely a deliberate point by Jesus (whereas Lazarus, the poor man, is named), matters not because rich people have a particularly elevated (or otherwise) place in the Kingdom of Heaven, but because of how this described his position in the web of human relationships. It seems to me that our human identity does, therefore, have some meaning beyond this world – if only because our identity ultimately points towards our relationships and the way we exist as social animals.

Yet we know that our human identities are anything but static. Our identities (and all of us have more than one) change as we change, but they also change as the world around us changes. We see this in the way we describe different generations (Gen Z's encountering of and envisioning of relationship is fundamentally different to even Millennials, let alone Baby Boomers), and in the way we change, develop, mature, and sometimes go off a bit (we are rather like cheese – sometimes ageing helps, sometimes it doesn't) as we get older! It is a hackneyed phrase, but our lives really are journeys, and because of this we cannot be surprised when change happens – we learn a bit more about ourselves, about the world, about the church, about those with whom we are in relationship, about God. In our learning we discern things by the season, and we find ourselves changed. This change might not be unidirectional – sometimes we might swing back, other times swing forward. One thing, though, is certain – whilst God is unchanging, we are ultimately creatures of change.

The risk we run, as humans, is that we mistake our own development, and discernment, the change that we find in ourselves through our engagement with the world and that others (dare I say, even God) cause in us, as the blueprint for everyone else as well. We find it almost impossible to imagine that other people might also have access to God, and that their relationship with God leads them to become different people to the people we are. Sometimes, perhaps, we are more justified in that belief – people who claim that God has made them racist, or misogynistic, or just plain nasty are probably barking up the wrong tree. Yet we know that they're barking up the wrong tree not only because it is obvious to us individually – and I would hope that it is – but because it is where our common discernment will lead us, if we read and meditate on the scriptures together, if we listen to the Tradition and are open to the Holy Spirit. Our collective connectedness matters, because it gives us access to something that is greater than our own meanderings.

You can somewhat imagine the scene in today's Gospel reading. The 'some present' sound like folk who might have sidled up to Jesus to give him some gossip. 'Have you heard about those Galileans whose blood Pilate had mingled with their sacrifices? Would you ever?'. Yet Jesus is having none of it – do you think they're somehow worse sinners than everyone else? Do you think they're worse sinners than you, because something terrible happened to them? 'No, I tell you, but unless you repent you will all perish just as they did'. Focus on yourselves before you start pointing the finger at other people.

There is something disturbingly urgent in the way that Jesus responds to the gossips in the crowd. Yet there is something else, too, which the original Greek reveals – the repentance that Jesus calls for is not merely a one-off, but a process of repentance. Any of us who sins (which, by now I would hope you know means you and me both!) knows that one-offs really don't do the trick. We continually fall off the wagon – our inability to keep our whole selves turned in God's direction, and our need to turn repentance into a continuous process is self-evident. So in Jesus' response, that we need to recognise the urgency of our repenting, and yet we also need to hold this repenting as a new way of being, something is revealed about the process of human life.

Jesus builds on this when he tells his parable. 'Sir, let it alone for one more year, until I dig around it and put manure on it. If it bears fruit next year, well and good, but if not, you can cut it down.' These are comforting words but words of warning, too. Much like the woman caught in adultery – saved from stoning, yet told to go and sin no more, we find ourselves faced with the mercy of God but also the righteousness and judgement. Yet importantly, like those who heard Jesus' words for the first time, it is *we* who hear them – you and I – and not someone else. Jesus is not telling someone else to go and sin no more (a depressingly common interpretation of the woman caught in adultery), he is telling us that. He is giving us due warning that God expects this from us, and that there is no time like the present to start the process. For we never know when we might perish; we never know when the fig tree will finally be cut down.

That might sound overly severe, but there is something important about recognising that God's mercy really might need us to hear that severity every so often. We have a patient God – a God who really does want us to turn again and be quickened. Yet we also surely have a God who is impatient – a God whose demand for justice for the whole created order means that our 'yes but not yet' (to paraphrase Augustine and his reticence for chastity) is not really good enough. It is always easier to see God being more merciful to us than God might be to other people – yet that really cannot be the case. Whilst we might struggle to reconcile a God that is both merciful *and* angry, if we see the primacy given to justice in the heart of God, then perhaps it becomes a little easier to understand. If God is a God of justice, then our refusal to participate in that future is stymieing the work of God, in however small a way. Such a situation is surely not something that a God of mercy can tolerate. We find ourselves, then, with a God who has mercy, but a God who has demands, too. Such a God is the God we find in the pages of scripture.

This may sound a little dour and unappealing, not least if we are hoping to follow a God who forgives time and time again. Yet such a God *is* the God that we follow. The Christian faith tells us that we are forgiven when we fall away, but it also tells us to return to God, to play our part in the bringing in of the Kingdom of Heaven. 'I said, I will confess my sins unto the Lord; and so thou forgavest the wickedness of my sin.' We will certainly receive mercy, but we cannot do so if we do not acknowledge our need for it. In such an acknowledgement, we find ourselves preserved from trouble, and compassed about with 'songs of deliverance'. 'I will inform thee, and teach thee in the way wherein thou shalt go; and I will guide thee with mine eye'. The question is whether we are willing to be so guided.

Yet it's not entirely clear that we can call ourselves

'righteous' or 'true of heart', simply for recognising that we are, ourselves, deeply in need of the love and mercy of God. Perhaps we are, though, able to – at least on occasion – find ourselves as those who put our trust in the Lord, and thus receive mercy embracing us 'on every side'. Every so often, we probably are 'like to horse and mule, which have no understanding; whose mouths must be held with bit and bridle, else they will not obey thee', yet in our process of developing throughout our lives, despite the stumbles, there will also be moments whereby we do not hold our tongue, and where our unrighteousness is forgiven and our sin is covered. And if we are like that, then perhaps we might learn to accept that others are, too.

To return to the theme of holiness, perhaps this is what being holy is all about – a process in which we find ourselves blessed, not because of our endless righteousness or our pureness of heart, but because of our willingness to return to the Lord and seek God's mercy, time after time. Perhaps it is that which is the process of sanctification – of becoming holy. Perhaps it is such a process that will follow us all the days of our lives and into the hereafter.

Our Orthodox siblings place far more of an emphasis on this sanctification, or deification, than we do – with its ultimate destination being union with God (*theosis,* a focus on the partaking in the divine nature of God). It is nonetheless surely that to which we are all called, however we might describe it. None of us is sinless, and none of us has a seamless movement towards that union – but each of us is called to an intentional, deliberate process of conformation to God, through the gift of the Holy

Spirit. In this process, in this journey of becoming, we are called to share in and, just as importantly, participate in the life of God, a life won for us freely and beautifully – gracefully. It is to that fulness of life that journey day by day, and our Lenten discipline will surely play a part in our hearing that call more clearly.

Questions for discussion

- What does 'holiness' mean? How might we find it in other people?

- Where might you have seen the signs of surprising holiness?

- Where do you derive your identity from?

- To what extent is repentance a process in your life?

- How might you see signs of sanctification? Where might you look?

- How do you square an angry and a merciful God?

- How urgent is repentance for you?

- How might walking the way of the cross be the way of life and peace?

The Third Sunday of Lent

Prayer

Almighty God,
whose most dear Son went not up to joy but
first he suffered pain,
and entered not into glory before he was crucified:
mercifully grant that we, walking in the way of the cross,
may find it none other than the way of life and peace;
through Jesus Christ your Son our Lord,
who is alive and reigns with you,
in the unity of the Holy Spirit,
one God, now and for ever.

Chapter 6

The Fourth Sunday of Lent, Laetare: Abundance

THOU, O GOD, ART praised in Sion; and
unto thee shall the vow be performed in
Jerusalem.

Thou that hearest the prayer, unto thee shall all
flesh come.

My misdeeds prevail against me: O be thou
merciful unto our sins.

Blessed is the man whom thou choosest, and
receivest unto thee: he shall dwell in thy court,
and shall be satisfied with the pleasures of thy
house, even of thy holy temple.

Thou shalt show us wonderful things in thy
righteousness, O God of our salvation; thou that
art the hope of all the ends of the earth, and of
them that remain in the broad sea.

Who in his strength setteth fast the mountains,
and is girded about with power.

Who stilleth the raging of the sea, and the noise

of his waves, and the madness of the peoples.
They also that dwell in the uttermost parts of
the earth shall be afraid at thy tokens, thou
that makest the outgoings of the morning and
evening to praise thee.
Thou visitest the earth, and blessest it; thou
makest it very plenteous.
The river of God is full of water: thou preparest
their corn, for so thou providest
for the earth.
Thou waterest her furrows; thou sendest rain
into the little valleys thereof; thou makest it soft
with the drops of rain, and blessest the
increase of it.
Thou crownest the year with thy goodness; and
thy clouds drop fatness.
They shall drop upon the dwellings of the
wilderness; and the little hills shall rejoice on
every side.
The folds shall be full of sheep; the valleys also
shall stand so thick with corn, that they shall
laugh and sing.

Psalm 65

Now all the tax collectors and sinners were coming near to listen to him. And the Pharisees and the scribes were grumbling and saying, 'This fellow welcomes sinners and eats with them.'

So he told them this parable:

82

The Fourth Sunday of Lent, Laetare

'There was a man who had two sons. The younger of them said to his father, "Father, give me the share of the wealth that will belong to me." So he divided his assets between them. A few days later the younger son gathered all he had and traveled to a distant region, and there he squandered his wealth in dissolute living. When he had spent everything, a severe famine took place throughout that region, and he began to be in need. So he went and hired himself out to one of the citizens of that region, who sent him to his fields to feed the pigs. He would gladly have filled his stomach with the pods that the pigs were eating, and no one gave him anything. But when he came to his senses he said, 'How many of my father's hired hands have bread enough and to spare, but here I am dying of hunger! I will get up and go to my father, and I will say to him, "Father, I have sinned against heaven and before you; I am no longer worthy to be called your son; treat me like one of your hired hands." So he set off and went to his father. But while he was still far off, his father saw him and was filled with compassion; he ran and put his arms around him and kissed him. Then the son said to him, "Father, I have sinned against heaven and before you; I am no longer worthy to be called your son." But the father said to his slaves, "Quickly, bring out a robe—the best one—and put it on him; put a ring on his finger and sandals on his feet. And get the fatted calf and kill it, and let us eat and celebrate, for this son of mine was dead and is alive again; he was lost and is found!" And they began to celebrate.

'Now his elder son was in the field, and as he came and approached the house, he heard music and dancing. He called one of the slaves and asked what was going on. He replied, "Your brother has come, and your father has killed the fatted calf because he has got him back safe and sound." Then he became angry and refused to go in. His father came out and began to plead with him. But he answered his father, "Listen! For all these years I have been working like a slave for you, and I have never disobeyed your command, yet you have never given me even a young goat so that I might celebrate with my friends. But when this son of yours came back, who has devoured your assets with prostitutes, you killed the fatted calf for him!" Then the father said to him, "Son, you are always with me, and all that is mine is yours. But we had to celebrate and rejoice, because this brother of yours was dead and has come to life; he was lost and has been found."'

Luke 15:1-3, 11b-32

Believing in God can be difficult.

That's perhaps a bit of an obvious statement. Even for the most committed Christians, there are moments of doubt, and moments even of disbelief. There are times when the story we profess is one we struggle to really internalise, and when saying we believe something, we hope nobody asks too many difficult questions in case we are found out. For a religion that is ultimately propositional, that says something about God – who and what God is, who and what the person of Jesus Christ is, that has creeds and councils and doctrines and dogmas – it's not simple to accept and believe some things and not others.

The Fourth Sunday of Lent, Laetare

It's for this reason that Christianity can be tricky, and maybe why it is so easy for us to break off into tribes, with our own particular version of Christianity becoming the only one we're willing to countenance. Paul, of course, had something to say about this (we might think of 1 Corinthians 1:12, amongst other places), but it does sometimes feel like an inevitable consequence of a religion whose understanding of God then feeds its understanding of humankind more generally. So we find ourselves in somewhat strange and rather sad situations – our identity as 'Evangelical' or 'Liberal' or 'Catholic' becomes more important than our identity as merely 'Christian'. In the contemporary church, it goes even further – we start to be defined as being, for example, the 'right kind of' Evangelical, one who has all the 'right' beliefs about a circumscribed group of things, and without them we are outside the camp. Sometimes it is we ourselves who make these tribal identities central to who and what we are; more often, perhaps, it is other people who do it for us.

These kind of 'in' and 'out' groups can become incredibly powerful, and with that power they can do significant damage to our cohesion as Christians. Much is made of the scandal of disunity in the wider church – between Catholic and Protestant, Orthodox and Reformed. Yet even within my own church, the Church of England, these camps hold significant sway. Sometimes they centre on people's beliefs – sometimes they centre on practices. Very rarely do they centre on God – very rarely do they start by naming the other as a Christian first, and then seeking to understand their experience and beloved-ness by God from that clear starting point. So often, we are simply unable to bring ourselves to believe that someone else might have the relationship with God that we feel we do – maybe out of fear that our own is too fragile and tentative.

The one thing that we Christians do know about ourselves, if we are honest, is that we are seriously, impressively good at judging others – and particularly our co-religionists, our fellow Christians. 'Judge not, lest ye be judged' sounds good on paper, but how many of us are really able to say, hand on heart, that we *do* that? Like the tax collectors in today's Gospel, we might find ourselves saying 'this fellow welcomes sinners and eats with them' with some disdain – yet because we do not have Jesus in front of us doing just that, we might be tempted to exclaim the corollary – surely Jesus does *not* welcome sinners and eat with them. For the Pharisees and scribes, seeing what was before their eyes made them question the identity of Jesus; for us, believing what we do about Jesus and our relationship with him, it is more that we refuse to countenance that such a sight would be possible in the first place.

The problem is, that is to rather misunderstand the ministry of Jesus. As St Luke tells us, Jesus says 'those who are well have no need of a physician but those who are sick; I have not come to call the righteous but sinners to repentance' (Luke 5:31-32). Those of us who are Christians know – or at least should know – that it is into that latter category, sinners, that we all fall. We are held in the righteousness of God, but not on our own, however much we might forget that at times. But oh, the cry will go up, of course we are all sinners, but it is not the being sinners that is the issue here, but being *unrepentant* sinners – it is the fact that *those others* continue in their sin, in their false beliefs, in their not being quite like us. It is in that, in their refusal to see and hear the Jesus that we see and hear, that the problem lies. Of course Jesus loves them – but they need to change.

There is some truth to this position, of course. We are not to remain static once we hear the call of the Lord – we are called to *metanoia*, to conversion in heart and soul and mind and body. We are called to reorient ourselves, to be transformed. We are called to put away our sins. All that is, of course, well and true, and is a helpful corrective when we rely too much on the 'God loves you as you are' narrative that has quite some cultural purchase. Yes, God does love you as you are – God also wills to love you into *metanoia*. God desires you to become more fully yourself, bathed in the sunlight of holiness. Yet the problem arises when we fail to see that the conditions are not ours to lay out – the holiness of life is not ours to define. We really may struggle to see that *metanoia* in another, but the good news is that it's not for us to see.

From the very first pages of Genesis, we have been determined to put ourselves in the place of God. Our wilfulness takes many forms, but the writer of Genesis makes it clear that chief amongst our first temptations was to eat of the tree of knowledge of good and evil – to put ourselves into the place of judgement. Eating from this tree gives us power, gives us authority. We know, of course, where that story ends – and yet we seem unwilling to learn and inwardly digest the consequences. Still, we look on others and decide whether they are 'real' Christians or not. Still, we refuse to leave God's things to God.

Perhaps underlying this way we treat our fellow believers is actually an anxiety, a concern that there might not be quite enough of God to go around. Our endless human need for competition might be the thing that leaks into our spiritual lives, revealing what is ultimately a lack of confidence – even a lack of faith. Not only is God unjust to reward others who are more sinful than us, with less claim to the inheritance than we have, but such an unjustness matters because we might be swindled out of what we deserve and be thrown onto the dung-heap. 'Blessed is the man whom thou choosest, and receivest unto thee: he shall dwell in thy court, and shall be satisfied with the pleasures of thy house, even of thy holy temple.' But what, Lord, if thy holy temple's waiting list is full?

For all that we say about our being unworthy sinners, saved through grace alone, called to repentance and swept up in the current of holiness that streams from Christ's pierced side, there remains within our traditions just something of the 'just deserts'. However much we might claim that we aren't like the elder son in today's parable, perhaps we do – however much we might not like to admit it – feel his pain a little. 'Listen! For all these years I have been working like a slave for you, and I have never disobeyed your command, yet you have never given me even a young goat! But when *this son of yours* came back, who has devoured your assets with prostitutes, you killed the fatted calf for him!' How could you? How could you be so unfair?

For that elder son, what is rightfully his seems to be being taken away – given not to someone worthy of it, but to someone who has already squandered what he has been given. He has his chance, but he wasted it on 'dissolute living'! Yet out of what Jesus calls 'compassion', out comes the father, bringing out the best robe, putting a ring on his finger and sandals on his feet, bringing out the fatted calf to kill it, preparing a great feast. It is of little interest to the elder son that 'his' inheritance is really his father's – it is similarly of little interest that the younger son has somehow been 'found'. What is rightfully *his* has been taken away from him.

The thing we really can't bring ourselves to believe is that God is a God of abundance – an abundance that, if we let it, would blow our minds. How often we seem determined to ascribe to God our own human limitations – to see the things of God in human terms. How little we listen to the words of scripture that talk of plenteousness – of fruitfulness that we can scarcely imagine. 'Thy clouds drop fatness', 'the river of God is full of water', 'thou sendest rain into the little valleys thereof … and blessest the increase of it'. The God who we worship is not a God who only has so much to go around – God is a God who will satisfy all who are called with 'the pleasures of thy house, even of thy holy temple'. Even 'the little hills shall rejoice on every side', 'the folds shall be full of sheep; the valleys also shall stand so thick with corn, that they shall laugh and sing'. The hard thing is believing it.

There are a few different names the church gives to today, which finds itself at a kind of pit stop in the middle of the Lenten season. In the UK, one of these, perhaps the most well-known, is Mothering Sunday, springing from the medieval habit of heading to the mother church for the day. In modern times, this has been replaced somewhat, at least in the popular consciousness, with the more secular 'Mother's Day', which has its roots in the day off given to domestic servants to visit their mother church – often alongside their own mothers. The association with the mother church – that from which, in many cases, the abundant grace of baptism was given – has been mostly lost, which does seem something of a shame. There is, of course, something deeply important about the celebration of motherhood and earthly mothers, but so often this celebration has ended up reinforcing rather unhelpful stereotypes. As ever, in the church, there is a place for nuance – a place rarely set!

There are two other names given to today. The first is Refreshment Sunday, a day when the Lenten Fast could be relaxed for a moment (including the use of the rather glorious rose-coloured vestments at Mass). Make the most of it! The second, and related, name is *Laetare* Sunday. This comes from the Introit used at Mass, taken from Isaiah 66, and beginning with the word 'laetare' – rejoice! Rejoice and be glad, rejoice with Jerusalem – redolent of (and in the liturgy directly associated with) another great psalm, Psalm 122: I was glad when they said unto me we will go into the house of the Lord.

Today, then, is an opportunity to make the most of that relaxation in our fast, and to reflect a little on the extraordinary abundance of God. This abundance is not limited – we do not need to worry about whether we will get our share of the pie. 'Thou shalt show us wonderful things in thy righteousness, O God of our salvation; thou that art the hope of all the ends of the earth, and of them that remain in the broad sea. Unto thee shall *all* flesh come'. Rejoice in an abundant God – rejoice, and be glad.

Questions for discussion

- Are you worried that there might not be quite enough grace for you?

- Where can you see signs of God's abundance?

- What might be the consequences of believing in an abundant God?

- How justly do you feel the father behaved? Would you forgive the younger son?

- What is the role of compassion in justice?

- Which name for today most appeals to you, and why?

- How might you make the most of this Sunday's relaxation in Lenten discipline?

Prayer

Merciful Lord,
absolve your people from their offences,
that through your bountiful goodness
we may all be delivered from the chains of those sins
which by our frailty we have committed;
grant this, heavenly Father,
for Jesus Christ's sake, our blessed Lord and Saviour,
who is alive and reigns with you,
in the unity of the Holy Spirit,
one God, now and for ever.

Chapter 7

Passion Sunday: Service

THE LORD is my shepherd; therefore can I
lack nothing.
He shall feed me in a green pasture, and lead
me forth beside the waters of comfort.
He shall convert my soul, and bring me forth in
the paths of righteousness for his Name's sake.
Yea, though I walk through the valley of the
shadow of death, I will fear no evil; for thou art
with me; thy rod and thy staff comfort me.
Thou shalt prepare a table before me in the
presence of them that trouble me; thou hast
anointed my head with oil, and my cup
shall be full.
Surely thy loving-kindness and mercy shall
follow me all the days of my life; and I will
dwell in the house of the LORD for ever.

Psalm 23

Searched Me Out and Known Me

Six days before the Passover Jesus came to Bethany, the home of Lazarus, whom he had raised from the dead. There they gave a dinner for him. Martha served, and Lazarus was one of those reclining with him. Mary took a pound of costly perfume made of pure nard, anointed Jesus' feet, and wiped them with her hair. The house was filled with the fragrance of the perfume. But Judas Iscariot, one of his disciples (the one who was about to betray him), said, 'Why was this perfume not sold for three hundred denarii and the money given to the poor?' (He said this not because he cared about the poor but because he was a thief; he kept the common purse and used to steal what was put into it.) Jesus said, 'Leave her alone. She bought it so that she might keep it for the day of my burial. You always have the poor with you, but you do not always have me.'

John 12:1-8

'Six days before the Passover' begins today's Gospel reading. Lent is a mixture of many things, but today it feels like we have reached a pivot – the moment where our eyes, like those of Jesus and his disciples, start to turn towards Jerusalem, towards the cross. In the company of his friends, Jesus reclines, yet Jesus knows, too, that his hour is close at hand. There are moments of tenderness, of intimacy, of friendship here – but there are moments, too, of facing the cold, hard reality that is coming for Jesus. It cannot be too far from the minds of his friends, too – Lazarus, himself dead just a chapter ago in St John's Gospel, miraculously raised by Jesus, knows what it is to go through the valley of the shadow of death. Lazarus, the friend who knows more than any other in the room what is coming, reclining next to the Lord who has brought him back to life.

In James Martin SJ's *Come Forth: The Raising of Lazarus and the Promise of Jesus's Greatest Miracle*,[1] Father Martin lays out the intriguing idea that Lazarus may himself have been the one described as 'the beloved disciple' in St John's Gospel (and we notably find the moniker 'beloved disciple' only after the raising of Lazarus). This disciple, who is named only as 'the beloved', has commonly been thought to be St John, but seeing this disciple as Lazarus adds a whole new perspective to the events that are to come. Mary, Jesus' mother, will be taken not back to Galilee, but into the home of Lazarus in nearby Bethany. It is not John but Lazarus who runs to the tomb on Easter Day. When St Peter asks 'what about him' in the last chapter of St John's Gospel (the final episode of Petrine petulance), he points not to St John, but to someone who has already died once, making sense of the idea that 'the rumour spread among the brothers and sisters that this disciple would not die' (John 21:23). It is very fascinating as an idea, but of course we cannot know. What we do know is that Jesus' relationship with Mary, Martha, and Lazarus is intimate, loving, and holy – and it is at their dwelling that he makes his final stop before making his final journey to Jerusalem.

[1]   James Martin SJ, *Come Forth: The Raising of Lazarus and the Promise of Jesus's Greatest Miracle* (London: HarperCollins, 2023).

Searched Me Out and Known Me

The fifth Sunday in Lent, today, has been known as Passion Sunday for a long time, and whilst different traditions do this differently in the contemporary church, nonetheless the gear does change today. Today, we begin a journey whose tension will increase, and which will ultimately culminate in the marking of the most holy of weeks. Yet today, too, we are invited to tarry a while with Jesus at the house of his friends, taking stock and remembering that whilst the events to come will be ones filled with grief, with betrayal, with shock, with fear, with doubt, nonetheless they are events in which our salvation is worked out. We do not go up to Jerusalem bereft of grace, but filled with the Holy Spirit – a gift whose genesis is these very last moments of the man born to be King, yet the man born to die.

Many of us will know the words of today's psalm like the back of our hand. It is one of the Psalms most likely to be known off by heart and finds its way into many of the 'pastoral ministries' of the church. We find the twenty-third psalm at weddings, and we find it at funerals, too. We find it on the lips of the dying and on the lips of schoolchildren. It is so popular, perhaps, because it is ultimately a psalm of comfort – one that speaks to the accompaniment of the God who is ever present through all the changes and chances of life. Yet there is something compelling here in the psalm, too, that speaks to today's reading – that of the anointing with oil, and the preparing of a table. Here we see the loving-kindness of God – here we see something of the nature of God. The God we serve is a God of service, a God of hospitality.

Anointing with oil has meaning. In the last chapter, we thought about the abundance of God, and here we meet that abundance again. In the psalm, the author (here we might reasonably think of it being or at least referring to David) is blessed by the abundant welcome that he receives, to the point of his cup overflowing. David is blessed not only by being welcomed – he is blessed by being honoured after his journey through the valley of the shadow of death, a journey on which God has accompanied him. Being honoured by God is no small thing, and seems to turn the whole thing upside down. Who are we to be honoured by God?

Hospitality is a much under-loved and underappreciated virtue in the current age. Of course, we are often willing to extend hospitality to those who we know well, who we might identify with, who might repay us the favour, but ours is not a culture that might offer such hospitality to those who do not fit into that kind of paradigm. Think back to the Gospel reading from Ash Wednesday, and the words of Jesus: 'they have received their reward'. What benefit it is to offer hospitality and service to others if there is an expectation that they will offer it back to us? Is that true hospitality?

It is reminiscent of Jesus' teaching in the fourteenth chapter of St Luke's Gospel. Here, he talks to the Pharisees about not taking the place of honour and about the importance of humility. He talks to them, too, about not only inviting 'friends or your brothers and sisters or your relatives or rich neighbours, in case they may invite you in return, and you would be repaid' (v.12). Instead, he says, 'invite the poor, the crippled, the lame, and the blind. And you will be blessed because they cannot repay you, for you will be repaid at the resurrection of the righteous' (vv.13-14). We are not only encouraged to do this through the words of Jesus – we are encouraged to do it through the action of God. God invites us, entirely without merit, to God's table – God anoints our head with oil, and our cup is filled to overflowing. Surely, we are called to do the same to others.

How little, though, we seem to take this to heart in how we live out our lives beyond the church door. One of the most extraordinary things about the church is that it's one of the few places in life where we might sit down next to a total stranger, someone who we would otherwise have little or nothing to do with and might avoid on a street corner, and take their hand at the offertory to share the peace of God. What an unbelievable sign and symbol of grace that is! Of course, time and again, we are enticed to create church and churches in our own image – whilst 'middle class church' is unlikely to get 'fresh expressions' money, it is all-too-frequently the norm in our worshipping communities. Churches of the rich and comfortable resent being interrupted by the poor and discomforting. Churches (and dioceses) of wealth resent contributing to churches of poverty. We become so wedded to our social stations, to our propriety, that we lose track of what it means to be people that are gathered by God.

It's one of the reasons that recent initiatives to gather like-minded people together and call it a 'new way of being [the] church' can be so dubious. Of course, we must rejoice in any opportunity to bring people to church, to God, to experience something of the grace and holiness that God offers to all flesh. Yet too much of an emphasis on likeminded-ness surely starves such 'expressions of [the] church' of something that is so integral and essential to being the church – the fact that like-mindedness has never really been one of the criteria. If you are not in a church community in which you are discomforted every so often, to what degree are the people there being called by God rather than by human interest? If your church looks like your social group, your sports club, or your dinner party circle, are you being challenged to love those who God is calling you to love? If your church is first and foremost about your personal choice, where is the hospitality of God?

The words of today's psalm are couched in individual language but sung together – they are words gifted to the whole people of God. That whole people of God is a people that you and I are called to serve, imitating the Master who we serve. Much has been made of the identity of the woman in today's Gospel reading (different Evangelists present the story or stories differently, and whilst St John makes clear that the anointing is done by Mary of Bethany, the Tradition has frequently muddied the water to suggest that this is Mary of Magdala), but at the heart of the story is an act of service and love that speaks to Jesus' identity and to what is to come. Not only is oil poured, but Mary uses her hair to wipe his feet – an act of extraordinary magnitude, and one that speaks of service and humility before the man who is shortly to suffer and to die.

We often use the word 'humility' in our theological meanderings, and yet give it the air of 'decency' – we must be humble, but we must not be humiliated. Yet here the wiping of Jesus' feet is both humble *and* humiliating – Mary is willing to submit herself to humiliation in order to honour her friend and her Lord. We will shortly see the same humiliation fall to Jesus himself – in the Upper

Room, in the scourging, in the crucifixion. Our Lord is not someone who is only humble in a worldly sense, who merely empties himself figuratively but holds a little dignity back. Jesus is *actually* humiliated in his service to humankind – born in an outhouse, socialising with sinners, nowhere to lay his head, and executed and tortured, despised, rejected. Humiliation is not alien to God, and it can't be to us, too.

Our Christian service may, then, at times mean that we are called to put ourselves in places which feel unendingly humiliating. There is simply no option to stand on ceremony as disciples of Jesus, however much we might think a task or a way of being is beneath us. As contemporary Christians, we are really good at talking the talk, but how good are we at actually getting our hands dirty and getting on with it. Many of us might see our Christian service as 'enabling' others – whether that's financial help, or the ubiquitous 'moral support'. Yet there will continue to be people tending to the rashes and sores of the homeless, there will continue to be people called to sacrifice much more than they would ever believe in order to lift another out of poverty, there will continue to be those whose task it is to clean up the vomit from the church porch, or to stand in the place of another when they face violence and harassment. Within our church communities, our worldly hierarchies all too often remain – those who clean the church remain those who clean the streets, whilst those who do the church accounts are those who wear suit and tie to work. In our own churches, are we really willing to accept worldly humiliation for the Gospel? Do we truly believe that even in those moments, 'thou art with me; thy rod and thy staff comfort me'?

When Jesus talks of always having the poor with us in response to Judas's weasel words, this is not to suggest that this fact of life is one we should accept. It is, surely, to state that fact and call us to action. Mary's prophetic deed points to who Jesus is; Jesus' prophetic words and ministry point us to our calling into service. Our own acts of hospitality and service to the poor amongst us are acts of hospitality and service to Christ himself (as we see in Matthew 25) – Mary's act of devotion and love here is inseparable from the acts of devotion and love we are called to take out into the world. 'Therefore can I lack nothing', we read – and because we can lack nothing, we are compelled to go out and do the same for others. In doing so, we will surely find the loving-kindness and mercy following us all the days of our life – and we will dwell in the house of the Lord, being more truly ourselves, serving God in our neighbour, for ever.

Questions for discussion

- What role does 'propriety' play in your life and the life of your church?

- How do you feel when encouraged to be humiliated for the Gospel?

- What acts of hospitality have marked out your Christian life?

- How might you put Jesus' example of service further into action in your church life and your wider engagement with the world?

- Do you have any sympathy for Judas's question?

- How does Psalm 23 speak to you? What does it most remind you of?

- What might 'converting my soul' look like?

Prayer

Most merciful God,
who by the death and resurrection of your
Son Jesus Christ
delivered and saved the world:
grant that by faith in him who suffered on the cross
we may triumph in the power of his victory;
through Jesus Christ your Son our Lord,
who is alive and reigns with you,
in the unity of the Holy Spirit,
one God, now and for ever.

Chapter 8

Palm Sunday: Power

O GIVE THANKS UNTO the LORD, for he is
gracious; because his mercy endureth for ever.
Let Israel now confess that he is gracious,
and that his mercy endureth for ever.
Let the house of Aaron now confess, that
his mercy endureth for ever.
Yea, let them now that fear the LORD
confess, that his mercy endureth for ever.
I called upon the LORD in trouble; and the
LORD heard me at large.
The LORD is on my side; I will not fear
what man doeth unto me.
The LORD taketh my part with them that
help me; therefore shall I see my desire upon
mine enemies.
It is better to trust in the LORD, than to
put any confidence in man.
It is better to trust in the LORD, than to
put any confidence in princes.
All nations compassed me round about; but
in the Name of the LORD will I destroy them.

They kept me in on every side, they kept
me in, I say, on every side; but in the Name of
the LORD will I destroy them.

They came about me like bees, and are
extinct even as the fire among the thorns; for in
the Name of the LORD I will destroy them.

Thou hast thrust sore at me, that I might
fall; but the LORD was my help.

The LORD is my strength, and my song;
and is become my salvation.

The voice of joy and health is in the
dwellings of the righteous; the right hand of the
LORD bringeth mighty things to pass.

The right hand of the LORD hath the
preeminence; the right hand of the LORD
bringeth mighty things to pass.

I shall not die, but live, and declare the
works of the LORD.

The LORD hath chastened and corrected
me; but he hath not given me over unto death.

Open me the gates of righteousness, that
I may go into them, and give thanks unto the
LORD.

This is the gate of the LORD, the righteous
shall enter into it.

I will thank thee; for thou hast heard me,
and art become my salvation.

The same stone which the builders refused,
is become the head-stone in the corner.

This is the LORD'S doing, and it is
marvellous in our eyes.

This is the day which the LORD hath

made; we will rejoice and be glad in it.

Help me now, O LORD: O LORD, send
us now prosperity.

Blessed be he that cometh in the Name of
the LORD: we have wished you good luck, we
that are of the house of the LORD.

God is the LORD, who hath showed us
light: bind the sacrifice with cords, yea, even
unto the horns of the altar.

Thou art my God, and I will thank thee;
thou art my God, and I will praise thee.

O give thanks unto the LORD; for he is
gracious, and his mercy endureth for ever.

Psalm 118

After he had said this, he went on ahead, going up to
Jerusalem.

When he had come near Bethphage and Bethany, at
the place called the Mount of Olives, he sent two of the
disciples, saying, 'Go into the village ahead of you, and as
you enter it you will find tied there a colt that has never
been ridden. Untie it and bring it here. If anyone asks you,
"Why are you untying it?" just say this, "The Lord needs
it."' So those who were sent departed and found it as he
had told them. As they were untying the colt, its owners
asked them, 'Why are you untying the colt?' They said,
'The Lord needs it.' Then they brought it to Jesus, and
after throwing their cloaks on the colt, they set Jesus on
it. As he rode along, people kept spreading their cloaks

on the road. Now as he was approaching the path down from the Mount of Olives, the whole multitude of the disciples began to praise God joyfully with a loud voice for all the deeds of power that they had seen, saying,

'Blessed is the king who comes in the name of the Lord!
Peace in heaven, and glory in the highest heaven!'

Some of the Pharisees in the crowd said to him, 'Teacher, order your disciples to stop.' He answered, 'I tell you, if these were silent, the stones would shout out.'

Luke 19:28-40

If you have been, or are going, to the liturgy today, you will know that it is rather a thing of two halves. We start by remembering the adulation of the crowds, the triumphal entry into Jerusalem, and in Luke's version of events this is near to the house of Mary, Martha, and Lazarus that we met in the last chapter. Yet by the end of the liturgy today, we have heard the entirety of the Passion narrative, and we have dived headlong into Holy Week. The contrast of the emotions of the day is always quite striking – many churches will begin by singing hymns and hosannas outside in procession, walking alongside Jesus into Jerusalem, and yet by the end of the liturgy, the music is much more solemn, the mood has shifted, and we are in a Jerusalem not quite so full of exaltation and rejoicing. The reality begins to set in – Jesus is not merely coming to be exalted, he is coming to die.

Our psalm today is that from which those words

'blessed be he that cometh in the Name of the Lord' comes. St Luke's wording makes reference to this verse, yet it is reminiscent, too, of the greeting that met the birth of the Messiah all the way back in Bethlehem. 'Peace in heaven, and glory to the highest heaven'. The heavenly host, on that occasion, sang of 'peace among those whom he favours' (Luke 2:14), and today we hear the 'whole multitude of the disciples' echo that call, yet those very disciples are told to be silent by some of the Pharisees in the crowd. The words of that extraordinary riposte are then put in the mouth of Jesus by the Evangelist: 'I tell you, if these were silent, the stones would shout out.' Here comes the promised Messiah, the Son of God, yet he comes not to a city decked out in finery for his arrival, but to a city of swirling distrust, of religious antagonism, of discord. A city just outside of which he will be put to death in an extraordinarily painful and humiliating way. Yet a city where the world will change forever.

Today's psalm is a psalm of praise, but it is a psalm of trust, too. In it, the psalmist talks about being hemmed in, where he is kept in 'on every side', with 'all nations' coming 'about me like bees'. Nonetheless, 'the Lord is my strength, and my song: and is become my salvation'. It is hard to imagine that the whole of this psalm was far from the hearts and minds, even lips, of those welcoming Jesus into Jerusalem. By referencing it, they are making clear who they claim this man is. Here is the same stone which the builders refused; here is the day that the Lord has made; here is the gate of the Lord through which the righteous will enter. Here, too, we will soon proclaim Jesus not only as the One who comes in the name of the Lord, but as the Lord, as God. 'Thou art my God, and I will thank thee; thou art my God, and I will praise thee', gracious and full of mercy.

Found in these verses, too, is what is to come. 'I shall not die, but live, and declare the works of the Lord'. The culmination of this week for Jesus is not merely his death, as much as that must come and through which salvation will be won once and for all, but his life -a new life which will definitively and endlessly 'declare the works of the Lord'. 'The right hand of the Lord hath the preeminence; the right hand of the Lord bringeth mighty things to pass.'

What must it have felt like to have been those two, unnamed, disciples who were sent ahead into the village to find the colt that had never been ridden? 'The Lord needs it' seems to be an unlikely way to win over the colt's owners, but it seems to work, and rather than Jesus entering the holy city – his city – in a great parade, on horseback, perhaps, or carried on the backs of his disciples, here he comes, riding on a colt. We will know, of course, the prophecy from Zechariah: 'Rejoice greatly, O daughter Zion! Shout aloud, O daughter Jerusalem! See, your king comes to you; triumphant and victorious is he, humble and riding on a donkey, on a colt, the foal of a donkey' (Zechariah 9:9). Yet there is another intriguing verse we might think of, too, in the Book of Exodus, where those things that are firstborn are 'set apart to the Lord' (Exodus 13:12). Here, we find that 'every firstborn donkey you shall redeem with a sheep ... every firstborn male among your children you shall redeem' (v.13). As to its meaning, the Israelites are to tell their children that 'by strength of hand the Lord brought us out of Egypt, from the house of slavery ... therefore I sacrifice to the Lord every male that first opens the womb, but every firstborn of my sons I redeem' (vv.14-15). Here, the 'Lamb of God who takes away the sin of the world' (John 1:29), the one who comes first, who baptises with the Holy Spirit, and who is the Chosen One (v.34), comes riding on the animal that the lamb will redeem, the Son of God coming to redeem the whole world.

There is much to muse upon in the imagery of the colt, but one thing that might not be so clear in today's world from this morning's processions around churches that would have made a much bigger impression in the early church is the order of procession. Nowadays, we are used to the bishop (or priest) being at the back of the procession – we implicitly recognise that processions go from back to front in terms of spiritual authority. Yet this was not the way it was in the processions of Rome – instead, the most powerful would come first, followed by their retinue, musicians, ordinary folk, and lastly the servants and slaves (if you look at some of the ancient universities, they continue to put the 'important' people first in processions). The early church subverted this model in a way that would have been quite shocking but has lost some of its saltiness in the modern age – it was an attempt to put into the practice the last being first and the first, last. I wonder what ways we might try to rediscover this in our contemporary church liturgies and practices?

The crowd shouting out praising the incoming Jesus did so, St Luke tells us, 'for all the deeds of power that they had seen'. Yet we know that the kind of power that Jesus holds is not the kind of power that the world is willing to countenance. Jesus' silence during the Passion narratives must be one of the most powerful actions that he takes, and yet in the mind of the world this condemns him. 'Do you refuse to speak to me? Do you not know that I have power to release you and power to crucify you?' says Pilate (John 19:10). 'Jesus answered him, "You would have no power over me unless it had been given you from above"' (v.11), unsettling Pilate. Jesus has trust in God – more than 'confidence in man', and 'confidence in princes'. He will be refused by the builders, yet will become the head-stone in the corner.

It is interesting that in recent years opposition to Christianity has once again begun to form, not because of the misuse of power and privilege that the church has so often been involved in (much to its shame), but because of its increasingly being seen as a church that 'takes the side of the victim'. This appears to be unsatisfactory – unacceptable – to many outside the church, who cannot stand the idea of a religion that is willing to subdue itself and shake off rather than grasp onto power. In a world in which strength and might are common currency, it simply makes no sense. Why on earth would anyone find that remotely attractive?

We, too, as Christians are anything but immune to that kind of thinking. Power, influence, and authority are both incredibly alluring and deeply corrupting. It is hard to think of a single generation, or a single tradition, in the church where the pull of power has not ultimately felt too strong for those who profess the Christian faith, and frequently for those who hold spiritual authority. It is not hard to think of the scandalous, shameful things which can result – the way that children, young, and vulnerable people have found their lives torn apart; the misuse of church funds for self-aggrandising; the all-too-close relationship to secular power. Each time, the essence of Christianity is lost, and each time deep damage is done to the lives of individuals, and to the life of the church corporate.

Yet one thing we cannot get away from is that power and influence are going to exist in any institution – and the church is no exception. What is needed is to find ways to live with, manage, and rightly order that rather than pretend it out of existence. Much has been made of the need to avoid 'clericalism', which so often boils down to little more than no 'Father A', 'Mother B', and 'Reverend C', but instead a rollout of 'call me Dave' and endless informality. This might work for some – but it is clearly not a satisfactory answer. Just because we might dispense with an honorific, nonetheless if the underlying dynamics don't change, then nothing has really changed at all. A priest with a first name only can abuse power just as much as a priest whose first name remains a mystery! Far too little attention has been paid to good stewardship of power, the need for rightful and enabling structures of authority, and healthy hierarchical relationship building. This is important from the house group level right up to the archiepiscopate – and into the world outside.

Deeper than this, even, is the need to ask ourselves how, what, why, and whether the power that is currently found in our churches is necessary, holy, and effective. How much of what we do is done because it's always been that way, and how much of it goes effectively unchallenged? What does a healthy ecclesial community look like, and why? What might honouring God look like in our homes and parishes when it comes to issues of power and authority?

Jesus' divesting himself of power and authority in

human terms ultimately leads to his reclaiming what is rightfully his in godly terms. It is to a godly, holy, life that we are also called – where what we do and how we act is in accordance with the people that we have been made as. Jesus' entry into Jerusalem is 'the Lord's doing, and it is marvellous in our eyes'; it is 'the day which the Lord hath made; we will rejoice and be glad in it'. As we enter into this most holy of weeks, what parts of our human lives do we need to lay down in order to take up those godly things and become more fully ourselves? What might be holding us back? Are we willing to enter in unexpectedly and find the mercy and graciousness of the Lord waiting for us?

Questions for discussion

- What is the place of power in your life?

- What does good stewarding of power look like in church and in the wider world?

- Imagine you are one of the crowd welcoming Jesus into Jerusalem. How might today's psalm affect you?

- What might the stones have shouted out if the disciples had been silent?

- What might God be calling you to lay down this Holy Week?

Palm Sunday

Prayer

Almighty and everlasting God,
who in your tender love towards the human race
sent your Son our Saviour Jesus Christ
to take upon him our flesh
and to suffer death upon the cross:
grant that we may follow the example of his patience
and humility,
and also be made partakers of his resurrection;
through Jesus Christ your Son our Lord,
who is alive and reigns with you,
in the unity of the Holy Spirit,
one God, now and for ever.

Chapter 9

Monday in Holy Week: Fear

I WILL MAGNIFY THEE, O God, my King;
and I will praise thy Name for ever and ever.
Every day will I give thanks unto thee; and
praise thy Name for ever and ever.
Great is the LORD, and marvellous worthy to
be praised; there is no end of his greatness.
One generation shall praise thy works unto
another, and declare thy power.
As for me, I will be talking of thy worship, thy
glory, thy praise, and wondrous works;
So that men shall speak of the might of thy
marvellous acts; and I will also tell of thy
greatness.
The memorial of thine abundant kindness
shall be showed; and men shall sing of thy
righteousness.
The LORD is gracious and merciful; long-
suffering, and of great goodness.
The LORD is loving unto every man; and his

mercy is over all his works.
All thy works praise thee, O LORD; and thy
saints give thanks unto thee.
They show the glory of thy kingdom, and talk
of thy power;
That thy power, thy glory, and mightiness of
thy kingdom, might be known unto men.
Thy kingdom is an everlasting kingdom, and thy
dominion endureth throughout all ages.
The LORD upholdeth all such as fall, and
lifteth up all those that are down.
The eyes of all wait upon thee, O Lord; and
thou givest them their meat in due season.
Thou openest thine hand, and fillest all things
living with plenteousness.
The LORD is righteous in all his ways, and
holy in all his works.
The LORD is nigh unto all them that call upon
him; yea, all such as call upon him faithfully.
He will fulfil the desire of them that fear him;
he also will hear their cry, and will help them.
The LORD preserveth all them that love him;
but scattereth abroad all the ungodly.
My mouth shall speak the praise of the LORD;
and let all flesh give thanks unto his holy Name
for ever and ever.

Psalm 145

Monday in Holy Week

When the great crowd of the Jews learned that he was there, they came not only because of Jesus but also to see Lazarus, whom he had raised from the dead. So the chief priests planned to put Lazarus to death as well, since it was on account of him that many of the Jews were deserting and were believing in Jesus.

John 12:9-11

We live in anxious and fearful times. Our geopolitics look uncertain – endlessly so – and our inability to find ways to live together that honours liberty but which balances this with our responsibility to one another and wider society is clear all around us. When there is scarcity, or reported scarcity, human beings change their behaviours and their attitudes – and sadly these don't often change towards being more cooperative or collaborative. There are examples, of course, of where hardship and difficulty has encouraged greater solidarity, greater sharing and pooling of resources – greater humanity. Yet all too often, we turn in on ourselves, storing away those things we have, and looking out for number one: ourselves.

Evolutionary theorists have plenty of ideas about where the collaboration-competition impulse came from – how favouring one or the other enabled human development at different stages in our ancient history, and how each remains baked into our way of being to the current day. Yet whatever the original drive, or the original benefit that might be derived from it, the depressing familiarity of human selfishness suggests that we have not yet broken ourselves out of this pattern of life. Human beings remain always teetering on the edge of putting the self first – even in times of plenty – and times of scarcity test our ability to fight back against this impulse.

Human beings, too, have another familiarly unpleasant way of behaving when we meet those who are not quite like us – who we think might pose a threat. Our willingness to think the worst of someone else, to look at them as somehow 'other', to feed our suspicion and mistrust, means that we are always on the lookout as to whether someone is part of the 'in' group, or a stranger. Is this person 'one of us' or not? Once again, there are plenty of reasons for this in our evolutionary history. We are, perhaps, hardwired to continue to behave in particular ways, as much for our safety and security as anything else. Yet in the world around us, we see what a heady brew this combination of behaviours can create.

Fear, suspicion, 'othering', selfishness – all of these are found in the very worst of human times, and yet we probably find them within our own hearts as well. Who amongst us has not hoarded something out of fear someone else might take it, however small that thing might be? Looking around at how we treat asylum seekers or refugees, or just those different from ourselves – how often are our fears built on anything other than fear itself? Clever politicians certainly know how to play on the fear of the other, on the fear of scarcity, and all too often we believe them. Our public services are overwhelmed because of all these immigrants, we are told – and whether that is actually true or not, it plays into our fear and finds us someone convenient to blame. It's a perfect displacement activity, yet it's also a perfect way of dehumanising our culture and letting us believe the lie that we have some kind of special entitlement to the free gifts of God.

The Bible is full of commands and encouragements to change this way of behaving, and yet if you look closely enough – even in the Psalms – you will find examples of attitudes and behaviours, even narratives, that seem to encourage it. This can feel tricky at times - it can even feel that when we read the scriptures, we meet a God who emboldens and incites some of the worst of human impulses. We need only think of the wars and devastation brought on the 'enemies' of God and God's people, or the willingness of the psalmist to wish destruction on those who are 'different'. Yet underlying these stories, we are able to discern a narrative that ends up doing quite the opposite. The Book of Leviticus is a good example of this – in Chapter 19, we hear the allusions to the Israelites' own slavery in Egypt, and a warning that they are called to remember this in the way they treat those from outside the 'in' group. 'When an alien resides with you in your land, you shall not oppress the alien. The alien who resides with you shall be to you as the native-born among you; you shall love the alien as yourself, for you were aliens in the land of Egypt: I am the LORD your God' (vv.33-34). There are many more examples, and it is on this deep, underlying thread of justice, openness, and ultimately holiness that Jesus draws in the New Testament (and it is important to recognise quite how antisemitic it can be to suggest that this is somehow a mere creation of the New Testament).

We meet fear writ large in today's Gospel. Poor Lazarus, who sometimes feels a little bit like a narrative tool rather than a three-dimensional great friend of Jesus! Not only has he died once, but here come the chief priests to try to kill him all over again. Far from the compassion that Jesus felt on learning of the death of his friend, the chief priests are reported to be angry because this dead man is no longer dead, and this is drawing people to Jesus. Being charitable to them, they might have thought the whole thing was a magic trick, or just a trick – that Lazarus had never been dead in the first place, but if they could kill him now then people would realise that *of course* this itinerant preacher Jesus could not raise him from the hereafter. Yet there is something in St John's writing here, too, that points us towards something deeper – fear. The chief priests fear Jesus, and his newly resuscitated friend – they are fearful of his influence, his apparent control over those things they know are rightly God's, his threat to their hold on religious authority and control.

They are fearful enough, in fact, to think that killing an already once-dead man is the answer. We met the idea that Lazarus might be the beloved disciple in Chapter Seven, but if he was not and he did not take Mary into his own home, then what happened to him as the Lord entered his passion? He, Martha, and Mary must have been terrified – he, a living and breathing threat to the authorities, and a painful reminder of the Jesus phenomenon, even once the Lord has been crucified. Would he really be allowed to go back to Bethany and live a quiet life? Or would Lazarus become collateral – killed once again, as a 'necessary evil', in order to forcefully reinstate the status quo?

Fear – and its curious bedfellow, ambition – can lead us to do things which we otherwise wouldn't dream of countenancing, and using other people as collateral, as means and not ends, is one of those things. We need only look at election campaigns to see the dispossessed used as political pawns by those who we might expect, temperamentally at least, to do the very opposite. When it comes down to it, we are always willing to put our own interests ahead of someone else's – to see others as an 'acceptable sacrifice'. The High Priest Caiaphas even says this out loud just after Lazarus is raised, exclaiming in council 'you do not understand that it is better for you to have one man die for the people than to have the whole nation destroyed' (John 11:50). St John puts a gloss on this statement, suggesting that 'he did not say this on his own, but being high priest that year he prophesied that Jesus was about to die for the nation, and not for the nation only, but to gather into one the dispersed children of God' (vv. 51-52). But then comes the chilling result of Caiaphas's words – whatever their provenance: 'so from that day on they planned to put him to death' (v. 53).

In our world we can see our 'acceptable sacrifices', and all too often we can see similar behaviours in our own churches, too. LGBTQIA Christians have been this acceptable sacrifice for years – 'just wait *a little bit longer* and we will see what we can do'. Prior to that, it was Black people, or women – particularly women seeking ordination. In many ways, it's not really in the past at all – just a little more hidden. Yet *unwilling* acceptable sacrifices become deeply inconvenient, and in so doing prove rather helpful as another deeply human tool – they become the scapegoat (itself an idea with interesting biblical connotations, most famously expounded by René Girard), the one who can carry the blame. Once LGBTQIA Christians, for example, are no longer willing to 'just wait' for any semblance of equality, then they become the reason that the church is splitting – the problem. In this dynamic, they either suffer in silence 'for the good of the whole', or if they refuse to suffer in such a way, then they are to blame – really to blame – for its downfall. It's an unenviable position to be in, yet with our human ability to 'other', it is not hard to see how it happens. Some call it out in these terms – like the late, great Bishop Alan Wilson did. Many do not – because it would harm their own chances of ecclesial 'success'. And so, the cycle continues.

What then can be done? What might be the antidote to fear, suspicion, and blame? What might help us escape the cycle of dehumanising others, denying their innate human dignity, and scapegoating them? Perhaps one thing is to intentionally adopt a stance of compassion. This is not merely 'being nice' – it is much deeper than that. It is about doing the hard work of challenging ourselves when we reach for the easy answers, and demanding that we refuse to turn away from 'the other' until we see the face of Christ in them. It is about recognising that we are lesser without them, whosoever they are. It is about going back to the source of the word compassion and embracing its original meaning – to *suffer with*. To be willing to put ourselves in someone else's shoes and to do so not because we are somehow better or stronger or anything else, but because we are called to affirm their human dignity in exactly the same way as our own.

This is hard work – but it is also God-shaped work. Today's psalm makes that clear – 'the Lord is loving unto every man; and his mercy is over all his works'. 'The memorial of thine abundant kindness shall be showed;

and men shall sing of thy righteousness'.[2] 'The Lord upholdeth all such as fall, and lifteth up those that are down'. There is much to be said for abundant kindness – not only because of how it might change our interactions with one another, but also because of the way it will change us, too. There is very much something of the holy in the being kind. Kindness can sometimes require us to be 'gracious and merciful; long-suffering, and of great goodness'. Yet it can also bring us back to ourselves when we are tempted down the line of fear, of closing ourselves off, of needing someone to blame. Sometimes an act of kindness can be the reminder to us that the way of compassion is possible. And that compassion might just open our eyes to the miracle of life, rather than seek to end a life for the second time.

Questions for discussion

• When do you feel fearful?

• Where might you be missing the signs of plenty in your life?

• Where have you been tempted to make another an 'acceptable sacrifice'?

[2] Of course, whilst the poetry of Coverdale is beautiful, the interminably male imagery is not! Perhaps this calls for an update to the psalter – to keep the poetry, but to lose the androcentrism!

- Who are the scapegoats in your life? In your community? In your church?

- How might you adopt a stance of compassion?

- What acts of kindness might you undertake this week?

Prayer

Almighty and everlasting God,
who in your tender love towards the human race
sent your Son our Saviour Jesus Christ
to take upon him our flesh
and to suffer death upon the cross:
grant that we may follow the example of his
patience and humility,
and also be made partakers of his resurrection;
through Jesus Christ your Son our Lord,
who is alive and reigns with you,
in the unity of the Holy Spirit,
one God, now and for ever.

Chapter 10

Tuesday in Holy Week: Doubt

PRESERVE ME, O GOD; for in thee have
I put my trust.
O my soul, thou hast said unto the LORD,
Thou art my God; I have no gods like unto
thee.
All my delight is upon the saints that are in the
earth, and upon such as excel in virtue.
But they that run after another god shall have
great trouble.
Their drink-offerings of blood will I not offer,
neither make mention of their names
within my lips.
The LORD himself is the portion of mine
inheritance, and of my cup; thou shalt
maintain my lot.
The lot is fallen unto me in a fair ground; yea, I
have a goodly heritage.
I will thank the LORD for giving me warning;
my reins also chasten me in the night season.
I have set the LORD always before me; for he

is on my right hand, therefore I shall not fall.
Wherefore my heart is glad, and my glory
rejoiceth: my flesh also shall rest in hope.
For why? thou shalt not leave my soul in hell;
neither shalt thou suffer thy Holy One to see
corruption.
Thou shalt show me the path of life: in thy
presence is the fulness of joy, and at thy right
hand there is pleasure for evermore.

Psalm 16

Now among those who went up to worship at the festival were some Greeks. They came to Philip, who was from Bethsaida in Galilee, and said to him, 'Sir, we wish to see Jesus.' Philip went and told Andrew, then Andrew and Philip went and told Jesus. Jesus answered them, 'The hour has come for the Son of Man to be glorified. Very truly, I tell you, unless a grain of wheat falls into the earth and dies, it remains just a single grain, but if it dies it bears much fruit. Those who love their life lose it, and those who hate their life in this world will keep it for eternal life. Whoever serves me must follow me, and where I am, there will my servant be also. Whoever serves me, the Father will honour.

'Now my soul is troubled. And what should I say: "Father, save me from this hour"? No, it is for this reason that I have come to this hour. Father, glorify your name.' Then a voice came from heaven, 'I have glorified it, and I will glorify it again.' The crowd standing there heard it and said that it was thunder. Others said, 'An angel has spoken to him.' Jesus answered, 'This voice has come for your sake, not for mine. Now is the judgment of this world; now the ruler of this world will be driven out. And I, when I am lifted up from the earth, will draw all people to myself.' He said this to indicate the kind of death he was to die. The crowd answered him, 'We have heard from the law that the Messiah remains forever. How can you say that the Son of Man must be lifted up? Who is this Son of Man?' Jesus said to them, 'The light is in you for a little longer. Walk while you have the light, so that the darkness may not overtake you. If you walk in the darkness, you do not know where you are going. While you have the light, believe in the light, so that you may become children of light.'

After Jesus had said this, he departed and hid from them.

John 12:20-36

We, all of us, will have struggled with doubt at some point in our lives. Doubts about our faith, of promises made, of loyalty, doubt about family and friends. We seem hardwired to doubt, as much as to believe. Human minds are a mixture of perceptions, emotions, behaviours, cognitions, each giving us a view onto and a processing of the world around us, and each contributing to the whole. Yet these ways of believing don't always entirely agree or entirely align – our heart might tell us one thing, but our heads another. Doubt can come about that has its genesis in ourselves, or in observing things about others that just don't add up.

Many of us may well have come across those strange creatures who seem to have no doubts at all – whether about themselves or others! Such people can be rather insufferable, unable to accept even the possibility that they are wrong. Similarly, there are plenty of others who appear to be all cynicism and nothing more, with an insatiable appetite to question everything. Sometimes there are good reasons for this. Endless questioning and even St Thomas-like demands for evidence are no bad thing in the sciences, for example, but when that takes over our lives – when nothing can ever be trusted – then we lose something of the relating to which human beings are called. Trust and belief are close cousins, and distrust and doubt seem similarly related. Throw faith and hope into the mix, and we get a decent glimpse into human relating and interconnectedness.

Because of belief's close association with trust, doubt sometimes gets an overly negative reputation. In some flavours of Christianity, it is essentially impossible to express doubt about or even question aspects of the Christian faith – and sometimes, and far more scandalously, express doubt about particular leaders within the church – without one's faithfulness to Christ or one's eternal salvation being brought into question. There remains at least a thread of 'trust me I'm a doctor' to Christianity, and whilst any religious organisation needs to have ground rules and some things taken on trust, in recent years the appalling abuse scandals have shown what happens when trust is not only unchallenged but *unchallengeable*. Sometimes doubt can be a very good thing indeed. As with most things, it depends on the situation, the people involved, and the institution. It depends on trustworthiness.

It's easy for us to point the finger at others who prove to be untrustworthy, especially when we have been hurt by their behaviour, their attitudes, and their actions. There are few things as skin crawling or painful as being taken for granted, being lied to, being cheated on, or being the object of a lack of trustworthiness. It hurts – it hurts terribly – and tomorrow we will think about the impact of betrayal on our lives together. What is less easy to do is to look into our hearts and recognise that our own trustworthiness is not absolute. Our own inability to rise above our wants and desires, our willingness (however much we might protest or minimise it) to throw others onto the bonfire in order to achieve our own aims, our own blurring of truths in order to get us out of a sticky situation or simply because telling the full truth would require too much work – all of these are true of all of us.

In other words, there is a reason that we doubt others – because in our heart of hearts, we know that we are just like them, and each of us carries in our hearts the seeds of untrustworthiness. Each of us is a reason for doubt. We will all have done something that gave another a reason to stop being quite so credible – so childlike, as we often call it, in their 'gullibility'. We don't have to be serial adulterers, to have fiddled our expenses, to have done any of the very public things that come back to haunt so many, to be someone who justifies doubt. We simply have to be human – and be honest about it.

You might think I am being a little unfair and stern – but perhaps that is because this hits home a little. *I* think I'm being a little unfair and stern – and that's because I know that *I* am a cause for doubt! The thing is, we get into patterns of untrustworthiness, and over time we become increasingly able to continue in a bubble that permits us to live with ourselves. Don't get me wrong – it really does seem to be the case that to merely *survive* in the world, we need to have a level of dishonesty in our actions – if only to spare blushes or hard feelings, or to get by in a world which allows us to thrive in the grey area. Yet our unwillingness to look into our souls and admit that this is the case is part of that very crisis of honesty. We don't like to see ourselves as anything but ultimately good – however Augustinian we claim to be, and however much we might state our belief in the doctrine of original sin. If not good, then at least trustworthy. At least someone worthy of a default of belief, and not doubt.

The astonishing thing that the Christian faith proclaims is that, despite the very clear fact that however powerful our delusions they remain delusions, there really is a source of trustworthiness and belief. There really is such a rock – a place of genuine genuine-ness, a locus of absolute truth. That person, of course, is Jesus Christ – true God and true man – and *true* in the fundamental meaning of the word. Jesus, whose trust in God is so strong not least because the Father's trust in Jesus is just as strong. Here we find a relationship of true belief – a relationship built on foundations which are able to hold, despite everything that is wrong and hateful and dishonest and untrue being thrown at it. A relationship which embodies genuine interrelatedness – that speaks to the possibility of truth.

Tonight's Gospel reading speaks of Jesus' soul being

troubled, and just a few chapters later in St John's Gospel, we hear echoes of this as Jesus speaks to his disciples. 'Do not let your hearts be troubled. Believe in God; believe also in me'. This phrase was used at my father's funeral and has been used at almost all of those I have been privileged to minister at, and at those moments – moments in which the heart is breaking and grief and hopeless longing looks for balm – those words of simple believing seem to me to reveal something of the holy truth in our faith. They're not simplistic 'don't worry about it' words, and nor are they words which pretend away the bereft nature of bereavement. They're not pie-in-the-sky fantasy that makes you feel better. They are, though, words which state something to be the case – whether we choose to accept it or not – that God is that in which we might truly believe, and not merely in an abstract sense. God calls us into a relationship of belief, in which God is willing to take a risk time and again on being the trustworthy one in the partnership. Our *being able* to believe in God means that God really is willing to take this risk.

In so much of what we do in life, we quite simply do not understand the destination – and that is surely true of our life with God. We are desperate for answers, or at least for signs that answers are going to come. We endlessly grasp after the next thing, never satisfied with where we sit. We think that – eventually – we will be satisfied, but we're not there yet. We lust after control – often understandably so. We are dubious of the journey, and we are dubious as to whether we can really believe God will get us where we are supposed to get without our help. Ambition is not always a bad thing in and of itself, but in the church, it can become so ugly, so antithetical to the Gospel. Yet so often this kind of ambition seems to be borne not out of surety in one's own brilliance, but out of a lack of trust in God – an insecurity, a fear that, when all is said and done, we need to be self-sufficient, to do this all ourselves.

In today's Gospel, we hear words of glorification – of honour – of trust. Jesus, speaking of his own mission, is aware of the need for a grain of wheat to fall into the earth and die in order to bear much fruit. He knows that those who love their life will lose it, and knows of the truth that sits at the heart of the Father. He knows all this, and he knows it because he knows that he can trust and believe in the Father implicitly and totally. He knows that of all those things into which trust can be imputed, the Father is the one – not only trustworthy, but the source of truth.

'And what should I say: "Father save me from this hour?". No, it is for this reason that I have come to this hour. Father, glorify your name.' Then comes the voice from heaven 'I have glorified it, and I will glorify it again'. This voice comes for the sake of those looking on, and Jesus tells them that 'I, when I am lifted up from the earth, will draw all people to myself'. 'Believe in the light, that you may become children of light.' In these verses just a few chapters before he is crucified, we are shown the clear and unambiguous trust that Jesus places in the Father and the Father places in Him – and we see, too, the need for Jesus to depart and hide after such a public display of intimacy. St John goes on to say 'although he had performed so many signs in their presence, they did not believe in him' (John 12:37). How easy it is to leave this at 'they'. How much harder it is to realise that it is 'us' – and us still.

St John continues, 'then Jesus cried aloud: "Whoever believes in me believes not in me but in him who sent me. And whoever sees me sees him who sent me" '(John 12:44-45). We are left in no doubt about the relationship of Father to Son, and nor are we left in any doubt about the relationship of truth and trustworthiness that flows between the two. Here is humankind's trust in God writ large – a trust in a God who need not be questioned, not because questions might not be asked but because the answers given will always be true. Here is the relationship towards which we are all drawn – yet here is its rightful source, God, and not humankind. We might wish for such a relationship with our fellow humans, but we know we will not find it. Yet we are offered such a relationship with the God who created us, who loved and breathed us into being – a relationship in which trust and belief are rightfully ordered, and a relationship that acts as a model for our own – which speaks into the depths of how we ought to model how and who we are when we enter into relationship with others.

Yet it can be hard to do that. Today's psalm is intentionally jarring in a world beset by doubt and lack of truth – doubt borne out of experience. Yet God calls us to a relationship with Godself that we can really, truly believe in. It is a relationship, indeed, that we are called to really and truly believe in not because of who we are, but because of who God is. It is a relationship that will both 'chasten' us 'in the night season', but in which we 'shall not fall' because of God 'on my right hand'. It is a relationship in which 'my heart is glad and my glory rejoiceth', and in which my 'flesh also shall rest in hope'. 'For why'? Because God 'shalt show me the path of life: in thy presence is the fulness of joy, and at thy right hand there is pleasure for evermore'.

It is hard to believe this, yet that is what we are called to do in our life with God. The Christian faith tells us that despite our experience with everyone around us, God *will not let us down*. That is quite the claim – yet it is the claim on which Jesus built his willingness to suffer and die, and the claim on which God was glorified, and our Lord rose from the tomb, and drew all people to himself. 'While you have the light, believe in the light, so that you may become children of light'. Will we allow ourselves to take such a risk?

Questions for discussion

- What is the place of doubt in your life?

- When might doubt be a good thing?

- How does it feel to be another's reason for doubt and lack of faith?

- Where can you identify places of mistrust in your own relationships?

- How might God's glory be manifested in your own relationship with God?

134

- How much do you trust God? What might be getting in the way?

- What will be 'enough' for you to trust in God?

Prayer

Almighty and everlasting God,
who in your tender love towards the human race
sent your Son our Saviour Jesus Christ
to take upon him our flesh
and to suffer death upon the cross:
grant that we may follow the example of his
patience and humility,
and also be made partakers of his resurrection;
through Jesus Christ your Son our Lord,
who is alive and reigns with you,
in the unity of the Holy Spirit,
one God, now and for ever.

Chapter 11

Wednesday in Holy Week: Betrayal

HEAR MY PRAYER, O GOD, and hide not
thyself from my petition.
Take heed unto me, and hear me, how I mourn
in my prayer, and am vexed;
The enemy crieth so, and the ungodly cometh
on so fast; for they are minded to do me some
mischief, so maliciously are they set against me.
My heart is disquieted within me, and the fear
of death is fallen upon me.
Fearfulness and trembling are come upon me,
and an horrible dread hath overwhelmed me.
And I said, O that I had wings like a dove! for
then would I flee away, and be at rest.
Lo, then would I get me away far off, and
remain in the wilderness.
I would make haste to escape, because of the
stormy wind and tempest.
Destroy their tongues, O Lord, and divide them;
for I have spied unrighteousness and strife
in the city.

Day and night they go about within the walls
thereof: mischief also and sorrow are in the
midst of it.
Wickedness is therein; deceit and guile go not
out of her streets.
For it is not an open enemy that hath done me
this dishonour; for then I could have borne it;
Neither was it mine adversary that did magnify
himself against me; for then peradventure I
would have hid myself from him;
But it was even thou, my companion, my guide,
and mine own familiar friend.
We took sweet counsel together, and walked in
the house of God as friends.
Let death come hastily upon them, and let them
go down alive into the pit; for wickedness is in
their dwellings, and among them.
As for me, I will call upon God, and the LORD
shall save me.
In the evening, and morning, and at noon-day
will I pray, and that instantly; and he shall hear
my voice.
It is he that hath delivered my soul in peace
from the battle that was against me; for there
were many that strove with me.
Yea, even God, that endureth for ever, shall
hear me, and bring them down; for they will
not turn, nor fear God.
He laid his hands upon such as be at peace
with him, and he brake his covenant.
The words of his mouth were softer than
butter, having war in his heart; his words were

smoother than oil, and yet be they very swords.
O cast thy burden upon the LORD, and
he shall nourish thee, and shall not suffer the
righteous to fall for ever.
And as for them, thou, O God, shalt bring
them into the pit of destruction.
The blood-thirsty and deceitful men shall
not live out half their days: nevertheless, my
trust shall be in thee, O Lord.

Psalm 55

After saying this Jesus was troubled in spirit and declared, 'Very truly, I tell you, one of you will betray me.' The disciples looked at one another, uncertain of whom he was speaking. One of his disciples—the one whom Jesus loved—was reclining close to his heart; Simon Peter therefore motioned to him to ask Jesus of whom he was speaking. So while reclining next to Jesus, he asked him, 'Lord, who is it?' Jesus answered, 'It is the one to whom I give this piece of bread when I have dipped it in the dish.' So when he had dipped the piece of bread, he gave it to Judas son of Simon Iscariot. After he received the piece of bread, Satan entered into him. Jesus said to him, 'Do quickly what you are going to do.' Now no one knew why he said this to him. Some thought that, because Judas had the common purse, Jesus was telling him, 'Buy what we need for the festival,' or that he should give something to the poor. So, after receiving the piece of bread, he immediately went out. And it was night.

Searched Me Out and Known Me

When he had gone out, Jesus said, 'Now the Son of Man has been glorified, and God has been glorified in him. If God has been glorified in him, God will also glorify him in himself and will glorify him at once.'

John 13:21-32

'Very truly, I tell you, one of you will betray me'. 'Lord, who is it?' Today, the darkness begins to descend – and the reality of what is to come sets in. Today marks the beginning of the end. Today, someone betrays Our Lord, and we watch on horrified as the events unfold. Yet today, too, 'the Son of Man has been glorified, and God has been glorified in him. If God has been glorified in him, God will also glorify him in himself and will glorify him at once'.

Every story needs a villain – in fact, so many of our so-called 'human' stories cannot deal with the reality of human life at all. How much we long to work out who the good folk are, and who the bad ones are, when we read a novel, watch a film or a play. Who do we support, and who do we loathe? Who do we want to identify with?

Judas is surely the biblical character that no Christian would have in the top ten of those to emulate. Judas, the betrayer – the one who must be replaced as an Apostle after Jesus' death, the one who did the unthinkable thing and turned his back on his Lord and Master. Judas, the one who either kills himself, full of remorse (Matthew 27:3-10), or who buys a field with his earnings from the great betrayal, falls headlong into it, and bursts open 'in the

140

middle' so all his 'guts gushed out' (Acts 1:18). Neither is an appealing end, and very few of us would ever want to be called a Judas. How much easier it is to point the finger of shame at 'him over there'.

There is a thread in Christian thinking that cannot quite let Judas die and be no more – remaining unredeemed and cast away forever. Judas, who betrayed Jesus, is nonetheless sometimes described as being amongst those that Jesus takes by the hand as he breaks the chains of death and hell. Some Gnostic sources suggest that Judas's actions, in bringing about what needed to come to pass, are actually laud-worthy. Christian sources might similarly see at least something of the necessity of betrayal in the delivering of Jesus up to his passion and death, even the glorification to come. Judas is a tool but nothing more – so how can it be right that he suffers for merely playing his part, like a cog in a machine.

There is something attractive about that wish to rehabilitate Judas, but we must be careful – for our motivations for hoping Judas might be saved are surely deeper than a concern for the disciple who got it wrong. Our motivations, surely, are much deeper than that – whether we like to admit it or not, Judas is not merely 'him over there'. Judas is us.

'And it was night' is another one of those powerful, evocative phrases that we find littered throughout Holy Week. Judas's betrayal here is portrayed not merely as a symbolic action, not merely as something to fit a narrative. As much as John tries to finger Judas as obviously being one of the bad guys from the start (let's remember that at Bethany, Judas is described as the keeper of the common purse 'and used to steal what was put into it'), let us just consider for a moment that Judas is a disciple, a close friend of Jesus. Judas is not a cartoon character, but someone who has given up a huge amount to spend time with Jesus, to travel around the countryside with him, to playing his part in the bringing in of the Kingdom of Heaven – yet Judas is also the one into whom Satan enters, and the one who is willing to put what appears to be his own needs and desires above those not only of Jesus, but of his other friends too.

In our last reflection, we thought a lot about the role of belief and trust, doubt and untrustworthiness. Judas's actions today aren't easily characterised as those of someone who hated Jesus, who was always out to get him – in fact, they appear to be driven far less by his response to Jesus than by his own interior life. Judas is willing to do *whatever it takes* to put Judas first, and anyone who gets in his way is collateral. Judas's betrayal is as much, then, about Judas as it is about Jesus. We know, of course, that Jesus is the last person who would betray, and thus the least deserving of betrayal of all humankind. Yet this simply does not matter *to* Judas – what matters *is* Judas. What matters starts and stops with him.

One of the fascinating and endlessly attractive things about Holy Week is how much of human life is there – how so much of what is said can be applied, without much difficulty, to our own lives two thousand years on. Betrayal is surely amongst those things. We all know how painful it is to be betrayed – and how much more acute that pain is when it comes from someone with whom we are intimate, who we love, and thought loved us. It is to those occasions that 'and it was night' speaks. It is night not so much because we have been wronged, but because the covenant between us and another who we have allowed into our lives, with whom we have pooled vulnerability and let us defences down, has been shown to be a mirage, destroyed in a simple action that makes us feel that it was never there to start with. If they were willing to do this, did they ever truly love us?

Forgiveness is hard when we have been wronged – yet when we have been betrayed, how much harder it feels. Most of us in intimate relationships of any form might be willing to forgive even quite egregious poor behaviour, but when that bond of intimacy is broken – when we find out the uniqueness of the bond has been violated, or where we find another with whom we thought we shared a particular trust has been selling us out to another – suddenly that forgiveness becomes a whole lot harder. It becomes harder because so much of what we thought we shared turns out to be (or at least feels like) a mirage – a hoped for reality that never was. On what shared canvas can we work out forgiveness if such a shared canvas has either been shredded, torn in two, or shown never to have been shared at all?

'For it is not an open enemy that hath done me this dishonour; for then I could have borne it; neither was it mine adversary that did magnify him himself against me; for then peradventure I would have hid myself from him; but it was even thou, my companion, my guide, and mine own familiar friend'. These verses from today's psalm put into spare but heartbreaking language the pain that betrayal brings. 'We took sweet counsel together, and walked in the house of God as friends'. How could you do this to me? You – my friend, my companion – how?

Today's psalmist expresses a number of the whole

gamut of emotions that we might feel in this kind of case. First, the need to flee – 'O that I had wings like a dove! For then would I flee away, and be at rest', remaining in the wilderness. Second, righteous pleading and calls for justice – 'destroy their tongues, O Lord, and divide them; for I have spied unrighteousness and strife in the city'. Thirdly, put vitriolic anger – 'let death come hastily upon them, and let them go down alive into the pit'. Yet finally, after all of these, the psalmist reaches some kind of landing place, if not total solace. 'O cast thy burden upon the Lord, and he shall nourish thee, and shall not suffer the righteous to fall for ever.' Back he goes to a further denunciation and bloodthirstiness about those who betrayed him, hoping that God will 'bring them into the pit of destruction', yet he ends once again by turning his face towards God – 'nevertheless, my trust shall be in thee, O Lord'.

This is a hard psalm – the language within it can feel terribly angry, problematic, even ungodly. Should we really be singing a psalm about vengeance like this in church? Surely this does not chime with the reality of the God who is love and who calls us to forgive seventy times seven? How can such a God possibly allow us to speak these words, imploring death to 'come hastily upon' others? To use the hackneyed phrase, if we ask 'what would Jesus do', surely it's not this!

That is, though, to forget that not only might we be the ones speaking this psalm about and to others, but that if we wish to hold onto that as a possibility, then we must own the possibility that the words of this psalm might be rightly used against us too. The psalmist uses the word righteous for himself in a way that might rightly make us baulk! For as much as others have betrayed us, so surely have we betrayed others. Our betrayal may be overt or subtle, but betrayal it is, nonetheless. Not only do we betray our neighbours, but we betray God, too. We may not have handed Jesus over to the authorities, but, like Peter, we will most certainly have denied Him – if not denying our faith in our words, then denying it in our actions. For surely the authorities could have found and arrested Jesus if they wished to – the betrayal of Judas is not about what practically happens as a result of one simple act, but rather about what happens when an intimate covenant is broken. It is about what happens in their relationship – the relationship of Jesus with one of those given to Him as a disciple. It is in that fractured relationality that night is found.

So what might we as betrayer and betrayed do with this fact? We are surely not called to pretend away the pain that betrayal causes – yet we are also surely not called to demand the destruction of others when we know that we ourselves are as much Judas as anyone else. The Christian faith certainly points towards holiness, truth, and the perfect – yet it does not seek to deny the real, either. It demands we attend to this real – that we face it head on, and accept our own part in it.

We human beings are called into relationship – relationship with one another, and with God. This relationship is messy and difficult – at times we feel like we are doing the lion's share of holding relationships together, and at other times we know that we are being carried in the arms of others. We, all of us, will make mistakes; we, all of us, will let others down. On occasion, we will forget ourselves and our true nature, believing that we really have no need of the other, whether God or our fellow humanity. Such a belief is a lie – but sometimes we hold it with delusional intensity. Sometimes, we simply cannot or will not remember who we truly are.

Yet, like Judas, when we get it wrong the promise of our faith is that there will always be something greater than we are – a God who is glorified for never betraying, for never letting go. It is to that ultimate reality that we point day by day, a reality that is a truer version of relationship than all our broken efforts ever can be. However much we take the inevitable step of getting it wrong, God will not, and will be there to nourish us. 'As for me, I will call upon God, and the Lord shall save me'. Such is our faith – it is our call to live into that faith, a faith of relationship and holy intimacy. As we look towards Jerusalem, let us prepare to meet with Jesus in the Upper Room for his last few moments of intimacy with those who love him – even the betrayer himself. For it is to God's table that we are called – and it is in the stream of the overwhelming love of God that all betrayal will, somewhere, somehow, be healed.

Questions for discussion

- How does today's psalm make you feel? Does it make you uncomfortable?

- How does it feel to identify with Judas? What do you think happened to him?

Wednesday in Holy Week

- What might it 'being night' look like for you?

- What might reconciliation after betrayal mean in the light of Jesus' passion, death, and resurrection?

- What is the place of patience and humility in the rebuilding of relationship?

- What are the current impediments to you finding holy intimacy with God?

Prayer

Almighty and everlasting God,
who in your tender love towards the human race
sent your Son our Saviour Jesus Christ
to take upon him our flesh
and to suffer death upon the cross:
grant that we may follow the example of his patience
and humility,
and also be made partakers of his resurrection;
through Jesus Christ your Son our Lord,
who is alive and reigns with you,
in the unity of the Holy Spirit,
one God, now and for ever.

Chapter 12

Maundy Thursday: Companionship

MY DELIGHT IS IN the LORD; because he
hath heard the voice of my prayer;
Because he hath inclined his ear unto me;
therefore will I call upon him as long as I live.
The snares of death compassed me round about,
and the pains of hell gat hold upon me.
I found trouble and heaviness; then called I
upon the Name of the LORD; O LORD, I
beseech thee, deliver my soul.
Gracious is the LORD, and righteous; yea, our
God is merciful.
The LORD preserveth the simple: I was in
misery, and he helped me.
Turn again then unto thy rest, O my soul; for
the LORD hath rewarded thee.
And why? thou hast delivered my soul from
death, mine eyes from tears, and my feet from
falling.
I will walk before the LORD in the land
of the living.

I believed, and therefore will I speak; but I was
sore troubled: I said in my haste, All men are
liars.
What reward shall I give unto the LORD for
all the benefits that he hath done unto me?
I will receive the cup of salvation, and call upon
the Name of the LORD.
I will pay my vows now in the presence of all
his people: right dear in the sight of the LORD
is the death of his saints.
Behold, O LORD, how that I am thy servant; I
am thy servant, and the son of thine handmaid;
thou hast broken my bonds in sunder.
I will offer to thee the sacrifice of thanksgiving,
and will call upon the Name of the LORD.
I will pay my vows unto the LORD, in the
sight of all his people, in the courts of the
LORD'S house; even in the midst of thee, O
Jerusalem. Praise the LORD.

Psalm 116

Now before the festival of the Passover, Jesus knew
that his hour had come to depart from this world
and go to the Father. Having loved his own who were
in the world, he loved them to the end. The devil had
already decided that Judas son of Simon Iscariot would
betray Jesus. And during supper Jesus, knowing that the
Father had given all things into his hands and that he had
come from God and was going to God, got up from

supper, took off his outer robe, and tied a towel around himself. Then he poured water into a basin and began to wash the disciples' feet and to wipe them with the towel that was tied around him. He came to Simon Peter, who said to him, 'Lord, are you going to wash my feet?' Jesus answered, 'You do not know now what I am doing, but later you will understand.' Peter said to him, 'You will never wash my feet.' Jesus answered, 'Unless I wash you, you have no share with me.' Simon Peter said to him, 'Lord, not my feet only but also my hands and my head!' Jesus said to him, 'One who has bathed does not need to wash, except for the feet, but is entirely clean. And you are clean, though not all of you.' For he knew who was to betray him; for this reason he said, 'Not all of you are clean.'

After he had washed their feet, had put on his robe, and had reclined again, he said to them, 'Do you know what I have done to you? You call me Teacher and Lord, and you are right, for that is what I am. So if I, your Lord and Teacher, have washed your feet, you also ought to wash one another's feet. For I have set you an example, that you also should do as I have done to you. Very truly, I tell you, slaves are not greater than their master, nor are messengers greater than the one who sent them. If you know these things, you are blessed if you do them.'

Jesus said, 'Now the Son of Man has been glorified, and God has been glorified in him. If God has been glorified in him, God will also glorify him in himself and will glorify him at once. Little children, I am with you only a little longer. You will look for me, and as I said to the Jews so now I say to you, "Where I am going, you cannot come." I give you a new commandment, that you love

151

one another. Just as I have loved you, you also should love one another. By this everyone will know that you are my disciples, if you have love for one another.'

John 13:1-17, 31b-35

If you are at the Liturgy of the Lord's Supper this evening, as the priest or bishop prepares to take the bread and the wine into their hands to consecrate it, speaking of the night on which Jesus was betrayed, you will hear the words 'that is, tonight'. For me, this is one of the most powerful reminders that during these three days, this Triduum, we are no longer living merely in our own time – we have entered a time that is transcendent and in which the here and now combines with the there and then, and with all time – the time, even, of eternity. In these few days, we are called to participate in the events of Jesus' passion and death – events which are as real and effectual to us here and now as they have ever been. In these days, the most earth-shatteringly terrible meets the most piercingly painful, yet all the while these events are bathed in the light of the unthinkably beautiful. 'No one has greater love than this, to lay down one's life for one's friends' (John 15:13). Here, that greater love is made manifest.

Maundy Thursday is a day which seems bursting to the seams with symbolism and action. Some of you may have been to a Chrism Mass this morning, in which the clergy of the diocese (and often those holding lay licenses, too) renew their ordination vows. Today the Gloria in excelsis returns, the liturgies are full of gold and white vestments, striking a real contrast with the earlier days of the week. Some clergy get terribly frustrated with the Chrism Mass taking place on Maundy Thursday, often because of the sheer busyness of the season, yet there is something important and holy in this busyness, in this excitement, reminiscent of the busyness and excitement found in the preparation for the Festival seen in the Gospels. Today is a day when gathered around their bishop, all those holding the bishop's license are called to pray together, to celebrate the Eucharist together, and to commit themselves once again to the service of God's holy people. It is a time of fellowship, collegiality, and communion – a time of renewal and restoration.

For Chrism Masses to take place today makes sense not least because during the liturgy we celebrate this evening, we celebrate – amongst other things – the institution of the ministerial priesthood. Christ gives us ordained ministry as the vehicle of service – as those called to serve the people of God, and not to lord it over them. We are reminded, as clergy, that our priesthood is not our own, but rather a participation in the ministry of the Great High Priest and Christ. Each of us, whether ordained or not, is called to participate in the priestly ministry of the church, finding ourselves equipped in order to equip, served in order to serve.

Yet tonight, too, we celebrate the giving of the precious gift of the Holy Eucharist – the creatures of bread and wine that become for us the Body and Blood of our Lord Jesus Christ. So hectic and multifaceted is today that there is now an additional Feast in the church's calendar, Corpus Christi, created so that we might give due reverence and emphasis to this extraordinary gift.

Yet we cannot lose sight of the Eucharist today – it is there, casting its light over everything – the service of service that sits at the heart of our communion one with another.

Of course, it is therefore a curiosity that tonight's Gospel reading does not mention the institution of the Eucharist – although it does speak of the disciples meeting together in the Upper Room (albeit with an apparently different timeline to the Synoptic Gospels). In the liturgy of the day, we hear St Paul's description of the institution, but here in the Gospel itself, we hear a different emphasis – John's focus on the washing of the feet, the *mandatum*. Jesus calls his disciples to him, and takes the form of a servant – washing their feet and refusing to take no for an answer. He does so not merely to serve, but to show – to reveal – what it means to be a follower of His. 'So if I, your Lord and Teacher, have washed your feet, you also ought to wash one another's feet'. So, in churches and cathedrals across the world, priests and bishops take off their chasuble, tie a towel around their waist, and wash the feet of (often rather unwilling) parishioners.

Of course, symbolic gestures like this that come with no conversion of heart are of little worth, yet we cannot dismiss the symbolism of tonight's gestures out of hand. The Lord Jesus' own actions are symbolic – meant to show the way, rather than to produce any particular practical result, here and now. In our symbolism as Christians – a symbolism that remains powerful despite increasingly loud opposition even within the church – we are called to truly participate in that which we are called to symbolise. Our faith is built on the fact that symbol and reality are somehow interrelated in a way that is not easily or neatly sliced through – our words and actions have meaning beyond the immediate.

It's for this reason that Jesus washing the disciples' feet is an example, certainly, but it is more than merely an example – in the same way that what we do in church, and how we model our communities, is not merely an 'example'. When Pope Francis visits a women's prison to wash feet on Maundy Thursday, of course he does so because it is a symbol and sets an example – but he does so, too, because this act makes clear, makes visible and discernible, something that is *true*. Tears flow not because the Pope is setting an example – tears flow because the Pope is declaring something through his actions, that these feet deserve to be washed, that these people have the same innate human dignity, as any others created by God.

This is the life that Jesus calls us to tonight. 'Just as I have loved you' – a love that is impossible for any of us to emulate, but a love we can yearn to embody – 'you also should love one another. By this everyone will know that you are my disciples, if you have love for one another'. It sounds so simple, yet how difficult we know it to be. In a world beset by violence and hatred, 'love' can sound so unrealistic as to be at best flippant, and at worst cruel. How can we possibly be called to love when we see everything happening in the world around us? What kind of a Christianity is that? It's for the birds.

It's an easy place to find ourselves – where love seems to be the same as 'being nice to everyone', and hence of little value. Not that long ago, several presenters on the *Today* programme on Radio 4 bemoaned the continuing presence of 'Thought for the Day' because of its apparent endless parroting of 'niceness', and perhaps they had a point. Love is not the same as 'being nice'. Jesus' message of love was not one that was received as something boring and unchallenging Indeed, in Jesus' life and ministry, the love of which he spoke was not simply expressed in words – it was lived out in his miracles, his healings, his encounters with those on the outskirts of society, at supper and, ultimately, on the cross. Jesus' life was the embodiment of love – and being fully human and fully divine, he showed us that our own lives are called towards that, too – that we become more fully, truly, human by becoming more and more an embodiment of love.

For the love we are called to is a love that makes many demands – it is a passionate love, it demands our honesty, it demands our service, it demands our reconciliation, it demands our holiness. It is a love that demands that we face up to the sadness and brokenness of the world, and commit ourselves once again to the fierceness of God's transforming love that will not accept platitudes or a shrug of the shoulders in the face of injustice. It is a love that refuses to allow us to cover our eyes and ears to the hatred and discrimination of our world, but that instead pushes us along in our quest for peace through justice and friendship through hope. It is a love that will not allow violence or anger to have the last word. It is a love that calls us to be a new creation.

It is a love that demands our all – that says to us 'give everything you are to God'. It is a love that will not only transform the world but that will transform us, too – a love that will draw others along to the vineyard, however much they might protest. It is a love that calls us to profess our utter reliance on God and to delight in becoming more and more Christlike. For God's desire for us, God's love for each and every one of God's creatures, is so infinite and so powerful and so overwhelming that all we must do is turn towards it and allow ourselves to swim in its stream. It is God's love that will draw us into the vineyard – it is God's call to us that we might join that stream.

It is that kind of love that Jesus calls his disciples to on the night before he dies – on the night in which he knows 'that his hour had come to depart from this world and go to the Father'. It is this love that is manifested in Jesus' life – a love that we are called to manifest too. Jesus does not call us to mere symbols – calls us to manifestation of the reality that sits at the heart of the Kingdom of God.

And he does all this at supper. He does so in the simple human, intimate moment of eating together – of companionship – of 'bread fellowship'. He does so in a way that we can touch – that we can sense – that we can believe. In doing so, he transforms this most simple of acts into the eternal memorial of his precious death and passion. He transforms sacrifice, and he manifests holiness. He does all this in the presence of his friends, who recline alongside him – friends who will be called to participate in the changing of the world forever.

In St Matthew's account of the Passion, Jesus and his disciples sing a hymn. I wonder whether it might have been today's psalm. In the moments where he knows he is to be betrayed, to be handed over, where he knows that the end is near, he calls 'upon the Name of the Lord; O Lord, I beseech thee, deliver my soul'. He promises to pay his vows now in the presence of all God's people: 'right dear in the sight of the Lord is the death of his saints'.

'Behold, O Lord', says the saviour of the world, 'I am thy servant'. 'I will offer to thee the sacrifice of thanksgiving, and will call upon the Name of the Lord. I will pay my vows unto the Lord, in the sight of all his people, in the courts of the Lord's house; even in the midst of thee, O Jerusalem. Praise the Lord.'

With those words, the saviour the world submits to his passion and death – submits in love, in faith, in hope. So let us go into the Garden with Him, and pray.

Questions for discussion

- What emotions have you experienced today?

- As you go up to Jerusalem in these three days, what makes you apprehensive? Excited? Concerned?

- What concrete ways might you live into love in the coming weeks and months?

- What demands might that love make on you?

- What does it mean to love one another as Jesus has loved us?

- In the garden, what are you thinking? What are you feeling? Who are you listening to?

Maundy Thursday

Prayer

God our Father,
you have invited us to share in the supper
which your Son gave to his Church
to proclaim his death until he comes:
may he nourish us by his presence,
and unite us in his love;
who is alive and reigns with you,
in the unity of the Holy Spirit,
one God, now and for ever.

Chapter 13

Good Friday: Faith and Hope

MY GOD, MY GOD, look upon me; why hast thou
forsaken me? and art so far from my health, and
from the words of my complaint?

O my God, I cry in the day-time, but thou hearest
not; and in the night season also I take no rest.

And thou continuest holy, O thou Worship of Israel.

Our fathers hoped in thee; they trusted in thee, and
thou didst deliver them.

They called upon thee, and were holpen; they put
their trust in thee, and were not confounded.

But as for me, I am a worm, and no man; a very
scorn of men, and the outcast of the people.

All they that see me laugh me to scorn; they shoot
out their lips, and shake their heads, saying,

He trusted in the LORD, that he would deliver him;
let him deliver him, if he will have him.

But thou art he that took me out of my mother's
womb; thou wast my hope, when I hanged yet upon
my mother's breasts.

I have been left unto thee ever since I was born;

161

thou art my God even from my mother's womb.

O go not from me; for trouble is hard at hand, and there is none to help me.

Many oxen are come about me; fat bulls of Bashan close me in on every side.

They gape upon me with their mouths, as it were a ramping and a roaring lion.

I am poured out like water, and all my bones are out of joint; my heart also in the midst of my body is even like melting wax.

My strength is dried up like a potsherd, and my tongue cleaveth to my gums, and thou bringest me into the dust of death.

For many dogs are come about me, and the council of the wicked layeth siege against me.

They pierced my hands and my feet: I may tell all my bones: they stand staring and looking upon me.

They part my garments among them, and cast lots upon my vesture.

But be not thou far from me, O LORD; thou art my succour, haste thee to help me.

Deliver my soul from the sword, my darling from the power of the dog.

Save me from the lion's mouth; thou hast heard me also from among the horns of the unicorns.

I will declare thy Name unto my brethren; in the midst of the congregation will I praise thee.

Praise the LORD, ye that fear him: magnify him, all ye of the seed of Jacob; and fear him, all ye seed of Israel.

For he hath not despised nor abhorred the low estate of the poor; he hath not hid his face from him; but

when he called unto him he heard him.
My praise is of thee in the great congregation; my
vows will I perform in the sight of them that fear him.
The poor shall eat, and be satisfied; they that seek
after the LORD shall praise him: your heart shall
live for ever.
All the ends of the world shall remember
themselves, and be turned unto the LORD; and all
the kindreds of the nations shall worship before him.
For the kingdom is the LORD'S, and he is the
Governor among the nations.
All such as be fat upon earth have eaten, and
worshipped.
All they that go down into the dust shall kneel
before him; and no man hath quickened his own
soul.
My seed shall serve him: they shall be counted unto
the Lord for a generation.
They shall come, and shall declare his righteousness
unto a people that shall be born, whom the Lord
hath made.

Psalm 22

Then he handed him over to them to be crucified.
So they took Jesus, and carrying the cross by
himself he went out to what is called the Place of the Skull,
which in Hebrew is called Golgotha. There they crucified
him and with him two others, one on either side, with
Jesus between them. Pilate also had an inscription written

and put on the cross. It read, 'Jesus of Nazareth, the King of the Jews.'

Many of the Jews read this inscription because the place where Jesus was crucified was near the city, and it was written in Hebrew, in Latin, and in Greek. Then the chief priests of the Jews said to Pilate, 'Do not write, "The King of the Jews," but, "This man said, I am King of the Jews." Pilate answered, 'What I have written I have written.' When the soldiers had crucified Jesus, they took his clothes and divided them into four parts, one for each soldier. They also took his tunic; now the tunic was seamless, woven in one piece from the top. So they said to one another, 'Let us not tear it but cast lots for it to see who will get it.' This was to fulfil what the scripture says,

'They divided my clothes among themselves,

and for my clothing they cast lots.'

And that is what the soldiers did.

Meanwhile, standing near the cross of Jesus were his mother, and his mother's sister, Mary the wife of Clopas, and Mary Magdalene. When Jesus saw his mother and the disciple whom he loved standing beside her, he said to his mother, 'Woman, here is your son.' Then he said to the disciple, 'Here is your mother.' And from that hour the disciple took her into his own home.

After this, when Jesus knew that all was now finished, he said (in order to fulfill the scripture), 'I am thirsty.' A jar full of sour wine was standing there. So they put a sponge full of the wine on a branch of hyssop and held it to his mouth. When Jesus had received the wine, he said, 'It is finished.' Then he bowed his head and gave up his spirit.

John 19:16-30

Good Friday

There is a certain inevitability to today.

People the world over, Christians or not, have some inkling of what today is about. Today is a day of solemnity, of silence, of reflection – a day on which Christians make the bold claim that Jesus Christ, the Son of God, was crucified. Today is the day when Christianity shows its 'weakness' – where the power of God is stripped, beaten, whipped, and nailed to a cross. Today is the day when sin seems to get the upper hand.

Of course, we approach today, like every day, in the light of the resurrection, yet there remains something important about meeting today with a level of holding back that Easter joy. To reach the empty tomb, we must go through the cross – not merely perfunctorily, or as if it doesn't matter, but truly and fully. We approach the cross – we live through this day – because it really does matter. We see the Lord of the Universe put to death, and we are called not to avert our eyes. As Christ hangs there, thirsty, as the life seeps out of Him and he bows his head, as the Spirit leaves Him, we are called to keep vigil.

There is a sparseness to what might be said when looking upon the cross – a sparseness not just because the awesomeness of this day overwhelms us, but because there is paradoxically so much to say and to meditate on when we see Christ crucified. Today is the culmination of the ever-increasing tension of the past few days, a day when what had to happens comes to pass, and yet a day which many of us would love to wish away. We turn away not only because the themes of the day might elicit emotions in us we find too dangerous, or difficult – we turn away, too, because the of the sheer gravity of what we are called to live through today.

Some people find the celebration of Good Friday too much to bear – or overbearing. For some, the solemnity appears misplaced – the cross is the source of our salvation and so our mood should be one of rejoicing and not grief. For others, the pain is simply too much – the reality of human sin strikes right to the heart.

Christians have spent uncountable amounts of time arguing about the meaning of the cross. We argue about the mechanism of salvation, about what the cross says about a creating and redeeming God, about what the cross says about us. We stare on it, and we argue. Yet today calls us away from that: we are called to stare, but to be silent. To marvel before the God who is willing to do *this*. To kneel and to kiss those blessed feet. To lay all we are and all the world is at the foot of the cross, and know that the Christ is truly present amongst us.

We have spoken about scapegoating in earlier chapters, and it is to the church's shame that even on a day like today, the church has historically reached for yet another scapegoat. You may have noticed the rather blasé use of the words 'the Jews' throughout much of our Holy Week readings – a phrase which has done untold damage not only to the church's relationship with the Jewish people, but to our ability to see ourselves aright as well. Our need, our insatiable desire, to blame *them* – the other, someone else, not us – has seeped into our historical understanding of the passion of Jesus, to such a degree that we often do not even notice it. Despicable, repulsive things have been done in the name of Christ and his church, and amongst them is the way we have persecuted, hated, vilified, scapegoated, and murderously set upon the Jewish people. It is only in recent years that the institutional church has even recognised this as a problem, yet if we are honest we know that it is not even partially addressed. We may have removed some of the appalling prayers written for today, we may have begun to cut the link between 'the guilt' of 'the Jews' of the passion narratives and our contemporary Jewish brothers and sisters, but the way we speak of and think of 'the Jews' has not really changed. It was they who killed the Lord.

Except it was not – it was us.

The hard thing about today is to look on the cross with grief and sorrow, and rather than look for someone else to blame, someone else to find guilty, the bad folks in the Gospel to point a finger at and excuse ourselves in the process, instead to sit in silence and know that it is we who need forgiveness. It is for us that the Lord God did this. It is where human sin leads – human sin that clings to us – and it is this, too, that is the answer to that human sin, in the form of grace. The cross is both inevitable destination, yet also salvation. Yet God needed to go this far because of how far we had gone – how far we still go. God did this because we needed him to do it.

The Gospel from today is so rich, and each of the Evangelists engages with these last few moments in the life of Jesus in a different way. For St John, the focus is on the completion of the ministry and mission of Christ. The beloved disciple and Jesus' mother are given to one another in a new relationship of love. The scriptures are fulfilled. 'It is finished' – and the spirit is given up. For St Luke, we see forgiveness writ large – 'Father forgive them, for they do not know what they are doing' (Luke 23:34). We see the criminal who has been 'condemned justly' receive the promise of paradise when he asks Jesus to remember him, to re-member him – to bring him back together again. We see, too, the trust of Jesus in the Father – 'Father, into your hands I commend my spirit' (Luke 23:46) – and the trust of a Gentile centurion in the innocence of Jesus.

St Mark has the taunting of the crowd, like St Luke, yet here we meet a Jesus who appears unsettled, in agony, crying loudly, and uttering those words '*Eloi, Eloi, lama sabachthani?*' (Mark 15:34). St Matthew, too, probably following Mark's account, has a similar vision of Jesus, and those same words are used – words which, of course, come from today's psalm. St Matthew's account is spectacular after Christ's death – the curtain is torn in two, the earth shakes, the rocks are split, the tombs are opened, and the 'asleep' are raised. Yet those words of desolation are there – 'My God, My God, why have you forsaken me?'.

There are many ways of interpreting Jesus' use of this psalm. Some commentators see Him making reference to the whole psalm through the use of this verse – others see only this verse on its own. The interpretations could not be more different. The psalm in its entirety ends on a note of hope. The verse in isolation is a cry of despair – the call of Jesus in utter isolation from God. Which one we are drawn to, perhaps, says much about our understanding of Jesus' relationship with the Father – and about what we think is occurring on the cross.

There are so many different ways of thinking about Jesus' death, models of 'atonement', models of what this 'sacrifice' means – each of them models which will never quite satisfy on their own. We find models that emphasise the need for justice, and the anger of God – models which can feel uncomfortable in their strictness, in the idea that Jesus is punished on our behalf. How can this be, we ask, if our God is a God of love? Yet perhaps we are too hasty to do away with God's anger. If we say that God is a God of justice, then would that God not be angry at the way the poor are exploited, the violence meted out against the innocent, at the way wars never cease, the sheer sinfulness of the world – *our* sheer sinfulness? Must not a God of justice be a God of anger, too?

Other models emphasise the obedience of Christ, the restoring of God's honour through the 'satisfaction' on the cross that only Jesus could bring – not so much punishment as restoration of that which has been lost. Others speak of the moral influence of Jesus on the cross – Jesus as the very expression of grace and love that transforms those of us who gave upon Him on the cross. Still others look towards the ransoming of humankind – the buying back of we sinners from our captivity to sin and the devil – or develop this into a wider understanding of Christ as victor over the powers of evil, redeeming us from our bondage to sin. St Irenaeus focuses more on the 'recapitulation' of humanity – the reversal of the effects of sin, and the bringing of us all back to our righteous state. There are many others – including the ending of scapegoating in the writing of René Girard. All of these speak something into the story of salvation, yet each of these is surely not enough on its own.

Some of these will appeal to you more than others – and all of them sit within the wide breadth of Christian belief in the atoning sacrifice of Christ. Yet all of them do not let us away with pretending we were not in the room at the time – each of them first demands that we accept that we were – we are – active participants in that which sent the Lord to die.

And yet.

We know that this is not the end. We know that there is more to be said about the crucifixion than our sins. We know that as Jesus gives up his spirit, the world quakes in even more spectacular a way than St Matthew intimates. We know that there is hope.

The arguments about whether Jesus used one verse to say one thing or another rage on, but we – like Jesus – know how today's psalm ends. We know how today's story ends. We know what is to come. We are called to declare God's righteousness 'unto a people that shall be born, whom the Lord hath made'. We are called to declare the Name of the Lord, to praise God in the midst of the congregation. For just as surely as day follows night, so will the day of rejoicing come. God is faithful.

Christus vincit! Christus regnat! Christus imperat!

Questions for discussion

- Gazing on the cross, what do you feel?

- Which narrative of the crucifixion most speaks to you, and why?

- How might you keep vigil at the Lord's cross today?

Good Friday

- How might today's solemnity be transformative in your life, and the life of the church?

- What is the place of Jesus' sacrifice in all you are, and all you do?

Prayer

Almighty Father,
look with mercy on this your family
for which our Lord Jesus Christ was content to be
betrayed
and given up into the hands of sinners
and to suffer death upon the cross;
who is alive and glorified with you and the Holy Spirit,
one God, now and for ever.

Chapter 14

Holy Saturday: Waiting

OUT OF THE DEEP have I called unto thee,
O LORD; Lord, hear my voice.
O let thine ears consider well the voice of
my complaint.
If thou, LORD, wilt be extreme to mark
what is done amiss, O Lord, who may abide it?
For there is mercy with thee; therefore shalt
thou be feared.
I look for the LORD; my soul doth wait for
him; in his word is my trust.
My soul fleeth unto the Lord before the
morning watch; I say, before the morning
watch.
O Israel, trust in the LORD; for with
the LORD there is mercy, and with him is
plenteous redemption.
And he shall redeem Israel from all his sins.

Psalm 130

After these things, Joseph of Arimathea, who was a disciple of Jesus, though a secret one because of his fear of the Jews, asked Pilate to let him take away the body of Jesus. Pilate gave him permission, so he came and removed his body. Nicodemus, who had at first come to Jesus by night, also came, bringing a mixture of myrrh and aloes, weighing about a hundred pounds. They took the body of Jesus and wrapped it with the spices in linen cloths, according to the burial custom of the Jews. Now there was a garden in the place where he was crucified, and in the garden there was a new tomb in which no one had ever been laid. And so, because it was the Jewish day of Preparation and the tomb was nearby, they laid Jesus there.

John 19:38-42

In many ways, it is all over. Except we know that it is not.

Holy Saturday is one of those days of the year that is most difficult to explain to those outside the church. What precisely are we doing today? For some of us, we will be waiting for the vigil tonight. For others, we will be waiting for tomorrow morning. We will be waiting, and yet we will be waiting, watching, full of expectation, and excitement. Churches will spend today putting all the furniture back, getting ready for the Easter feast. Clergy will be putting the final touches to the liturgy. Candidates for confirmation will be being met and prepared. Yet through all of this, we wait.

Waiting is a hugely underrated part of contemporary life – though that is not to say that it is easy. We are so used to things being delivered immediately, to being able to find out what we need to know precisely when we need to know it, that the art – and I think it is an art – of waiting has become something we are simply unequipped to engage in. I will admit that waiting is, for me, a kind of mini-hell – I remember all too well the wait for exam results, the wait for things that I have hoped and dreamt for, that seem to take so long to come. Yet waiting can be so much more than that, too. It can be the dwelling a while and not being sure of what the next thing we are being called to is. It can be the lack of clarity over a decision. Waiting can be painful, yet waiting is part and parcel of life, however much we have tried to get rid of it. Waiting can be a time of growth, too, yet we ought not to overstate the ease of such growth. Waiting can sometimes just be hard work.

In our lives in Christ, this waiting can be very painful indeed. 'Where are you, God, when we need you?', we might find ourselves asking. Why need so many children die in a famine? Why are so few wars ended quickly? Where are you? Questions of theodicy – the need to understand God's role in the existence of evil – is something those of faith have been caught up with for generations, yet no compelling answer has been found. Instead, we sit, and we wait – questioning. We ask – and so often we hear no reply.

Suggesting there is something holy in such waiting seems to go against everything we say we believe in. It is easy for comfortable middle-class people sitting in their armchairs to speak of the sanctification of holiness, but for those on the sharp edge, such a position is all-too-often both cruel and unthinking. There is surely nothing holy about children starving, whilst waiting for food. There is surely nothing holy about the killing of civilians in an endless war. Such waiting seems the very opposite of holy.

Yet waiting is found in so much of the Christian faith – in the scriptures, and in the lives of Christians. Today's psalm speaks to this, and waiting on the Lord is found as a constant refrain throughout our psalmody more generally. How do we square this with the God of love?

Right at the centre of the Christ event, we find waiting. Here, today, at the tomb, in the midst of the grief and despair that must have enveloped the disciples, we find waiting. How were they to know that such waiting had a purpose – or what that purpose might be? Were they even to know that they *were* waiting? Yet wait they did.

Our frustration, our disappointment, our bitterness at God – which we all have, whether we admit it or not – can be found so often in our waiting. Our wait for justice, our wait for signs of hope, our wait for redemption. We look for the Lord, our soul waits for him – our soul fleeth unto the Lord before the morning watch, out of the deep. Yet can we hear the psalmist imploring us to trust for the plenteous redemption, for the redemption from all our sins?

Today is a day of waiting – and so that is what we will do, however uncomfortable or unjust it might feel. For waiting is part of the mystery of the God who will soon make Godself present in our midst.

Holy Saturday

Questions for discussion

- What is the place of waiting in your life?

- What most frustrates you about waiting on the Lord?

- How might you have waited and watched that first Holy Saturday?

- Where is God in all the waiting?

Prayer

Grant, Lord,
that we who are baptized into the death
of your Son our Saviour Jesus Christ
may continually put to death our evil desires
and be buried with him;
and that through the grave and gate of death
we may pass to our joyful resurrection;
through his merits,
who died and was buried and rose again for us,
your Son Jesus Christ our Lord.

Chapter 15

Easter Day: Redemption Through Love

LORD, thou art become gracious
unto thy land; thou hast turned away the
captivity of Jacob.
Thou hast forgiven the offence of thy people,
and covered all their sins.
Thou hast taken away all thy displeasure, and
turned thyself from thy wrathful indignation.
Turn us then, O God our Saviour, and let thine
anger cease from us.
Wilt thou be displeased at us for ever? and wilt
thou stretch out thy wrath from one generation
to another?
Wilt thou not turn again, and quicken us, that
thy people may rejoice in thee?
Show us thy mercy, O LORD, and grant us thy
salvation.
I will hearken what the LORD God will say;
for he shall speak peace unto his people, and
to his saints, that they turn not again unto
foolishness.

For his salvation is nigh them that fear him; that
glory may dwell in our land.
Mercy and truth are met together:
righteousness and peace have kissed each other.
Truth shall flourish out of the earth, and
righteousness hath looked down from heaven.
Yea, the LORD shall show loving-kindness; and
our land shall give her increase.
Righteousness shall go before him, and shall
direct his going in the way.

Psalm 85

But on the first day of the week, at early dawn, they
went to the tomb, taking the spices that they had
prepared. They found the stone rolled away from the
tomb, but when they went in they did not find the
body. While they were perplexed about this, suddenly
two men in dazzling clothes stood beside them. The
women were terrified and bowed their faces to the
ground, but the men said to them, 'Why do you look for
the living among the dead? He is not here but has risen.
Remember how he told you, while he was still in Galilee,
that the Son of Man must be handed over to the hands
of sinners and be crucified and on the third day rise
again.' Then they remembered his words, and returning
from the tomb they told all this to the eleven and to all
the rest. Now it was Mary Magdalene, Joanna, Mary the
mother of James, and the other women with them who
told this to the apostles. But these words seemed to

them an idle tale, and they did not believe them.

But Peter got up and ran to the tomb; stooping and looking in, he saw the linen cloths by themselves; then he went home, amazed at what had happened.

Luke 24:1-12

It is the women who first learn of what has happened to the Lord Jesus.

Like the narratives of the crucifixion, each Gospel writer gives us an Easter Day revelation with different emphases or shades of meaning. Yet each Gospel writer testifies to the same truth – that Jesus Christ is risen from the tomb, and with that, the entire created order has been changed forever. Each time, it is the women who come – and it is the women who are not believed. Yet it is to those unbelieved women that the truth first comes. It is to those who were faithful, who stood by the cross, who loved when others deserted. Will we be willing to hear them, and believe them?

Today, take time to read each of the Gospel accounts, because they each tell the same story through a different lens. They each speak to us of the reality that sits ready for us to grasp. For this is the central truth claim of Christianity – that Jesus really, truly rose on that third day. This is not metaphor, it is not religious imagery, it is not mere symbolism. It is, like so much of the scriptural narrative and our Christian lives, living symbol – actual, realised eschatology, life in the forever lived in the here and now. That first Easter morning, the women did not meet an empty tomb as an idea, or as a piece of secret knowledge. The women met an empty tomb because their Lord and ours had risen to new life, glorified by the God who he glorified. Today we stake all we have on that claim, because that claim tells us that despite everything – despite the horrors and the heartbreaks – love wins. Redemptive love is *the* reality of our existence – and is offered to us all, not primarily because we love God, but because God loves us, and has done since the moment of our coming into being.

What we celebrate today is no cheap grace. There is no resurrection without the cross, without the loss, and the anguish, and the piercing despair of that day on Calvary. This great Feast that we celebrate does not somehow wipe those things away, nor deny the realities that so often mar our own lives – the disappointments, the frustrations, the hurt, the anger, the betrayal. Yet this Feast turns to all these enemies of love, to all these enemies of the common good, to all these enemies of joy, and says clearly, and unmistakeably, *you will not win*. Death be not proud – death the great enemy, the very thing that says no to life and claims to end all things – death, be not proud – death, thou shalt die.

For the resurrection of Christ is the greatest act of resistance to those things that tear down, those very things that continue to threaten our world. Today, on this great feast, let us repeat and believe that for all their posturing, for all their determination to ruin and destroy, for all the power they seem to have on our lives, the ultimate victory is the Lord's! Christ has overcome! The world has changed! Alleluia!

The psalm we meet today is one of my favourites,

because it speaks of the world that really is – the world that God wills into being in the resurrection event, and which will be ours, when all is brought to completion. It is a world of graciousness and forgiveness, where salvation is not only nigh but granted to us. It is a world of reconciliation that springs from the God-given reconciliation achieved once and for all upon the cross, that can never be defeated. It is a world where mercy and truth meet together, where righteousness and peace kill each other – where truth flourishes out of the earth, and righteousness looks down from heaven. It is a world that is infused with loving-kindness, and where our goings are directed not by wilfulness, not by sin, not by all those things that beset us in this earthly pilgrimage, but by God.

Today and every day, beloved and holy disciples of the Lord Jesus, bask in the resurrection life, in the being known, in the being loved. Hear the words of joy, faith, hope, and love, that Christ speaks and realise they are directed to you and to the whole world. Go with the women and see the empty tomb, not meanly holding onto that risen life for yourself but sharing it with others, going into the world as his ransomed, healed, restored, forgiven people. Live lives full of the resurrection – lives full of holy, unremitting joy. Joy that endures despite all the world might throw at us, joy that infuses and enlivens us even at our lowest moments. Joy that invigorates a church and world riven by anxieties and fear, and which calls us into newness of life – life everlasting.

Alleluia, my dear friends, alleluia! Christ is risen from the dead. *Christus Surrexit!* Christ has made captivity captive, he has wiped away our sins, he intercedes for us, he accompanies us, he calls us friends, he adores us. he meets us – you and me – in the garden of resurrection life, and bids us not only to tell his story but to live the life that he gives us. He calls us into Easter joy – joy which bubbles over, which effervesces out of us and which loves the Kingdom of Heaven into being day by day by day. Joy which can stand the test; joy which has its source in the God who delights in us, delights in us *together* as God's holy people.

We have work to do, to participate in the life of the Kingdom, to put our hand to the plough, to commit ourselves to justice, and to peace, and to holiness of life. For this Easter joy is not yours nor mine but ours, and not ours alone but for the whole of creation. My friends, do not delay – Our Lord is Risen and the Kingdom of Heaven has come near. Let us find the face of the resurrected Christ in the Other, in the stranger, in the destitute, in the refugee, in the despised, in the abandoned, in the sick, in the marginalised, in the wonderful, God-given diversity we see around us, and in those the world and yes, we ourselves, so often ignore, and let us greet them – and let them greet us – as fellow beloved children of God. Let us be ready to play our part in the justice of God in our churches, our communities, and amongst the most vulnerable. Let us recommit our whole lives to the Kingdom of Heaven. The hour is at hand!

Alleluia, Christ is Risen! He is Risen indeed! Alleluia!

There are no questions for discussion today. Enjoy your Easter – feast, party, rejoice – for the Lord Jesus has leapt from the tomb, taking captivity captive. The Lord Jesus is alive and reigns forever.

God the Father, the Son, and the Holy Spirit, bless you

this Eastertide. Know that you were breathed into being in love and loved into redemption. Know that the resurrection changes everything.

Prayer

Rejoice, heavenly powers! Sing, choirs of angels!
Exult, all creation around God's throne!
Jesus Christ, our King, is risen!
Sound the trumpet of salvation!

Rejoice, O earth, in shining splendor,
radiant in the brightness of your King!
Christ has conquered! Glory fills you!
Darkness vanishes for ever!

Rejoice, O Mother Church! Exult in glory!
The risen Savior shines upon you!
Let this place resound with joy,
echoing the mighty song of all God's people!

For Christ has ransomed us with his blood,
and paid for us the price of Adam's sin
to our eternal Father!

This is our passover feast,
when Christ, the true Lamb, is slain,
whose blood consecrates the homes of all believers.

This is the night
when first you saved our fathers:

Searched Me Out and Known Me

you freed the people of Israel from their slavery
and led them dry-shod through the sea.

This is the night
when the pillar of fire destroyed the darkness of sin!

This is the night
when Christians everywhere,
washed clean of sin and freed from all defilement,
are restored to grace and grow together in holiness.
This is the night
when Jesus Christ broke the chains of death
and rose triumphant from the grave.

What good would life have been to us,
had Christ not come as our Redeemer?
Father, how wonderful your care for us!
How boundless your merciful love!
To ransom a slave you gave away your Son.

O happy fault,
O necessary sin of Adam,
which gained for us so great a Redeemer!

Most blessed of all nights,
chosen by God to see Christ rising from the dead!

Of this night scripture says:
'The night will be as clear as day:
it will become my light, my joy.'
The power of this holy night dispels all evil,
washes guilt away, restores lost innocence,

Easter Day

brings mourners joy;
it casts out hatred, brings us peace,
and humbles earthly pride.

Night truly blessed when heaven is wedded to earth
and man is reconciled with God!

Therefore, heavenly Father,
in the joy of this night,
receive our evening sacrifice of praise,
your Church's solemn offering.

Accept this Easter candle,
a flame divided but undimmed,
a pillar of fire that glows to the honor of God.

Let it mingle with the lights of heaven
and continue bravely burning
to dispel the darkness of this night!

May the Morning Star which never sets
find this flame still burning:
Christ, that Morning Star,
who came back from the dead,
and shed his peaceful light on all mankind,
your Son, who lives and reigns for ever and ever.
Amen.[3]

---

[3] The Exultet, words as used at the Monastery of Bose,
available here: https://www.monasterodibose.it/en/prayer/
prayers/3155-rejoice-heavenly-powers-sing-choirs-of-angels
[accessed August 10th 2024].

Searched Me Out and Known Me

Lord of all life and power,
who through the mighty resurrection of your Son
overcame the old order of sin and death
to make all things new in him:
grant that we, being dead to sin
and alive to you in Jesus Christ,
may reign with him in glory;
to whom with you and the Holy Spirit
be praise and honour, glory and might,
now and in all eternity.